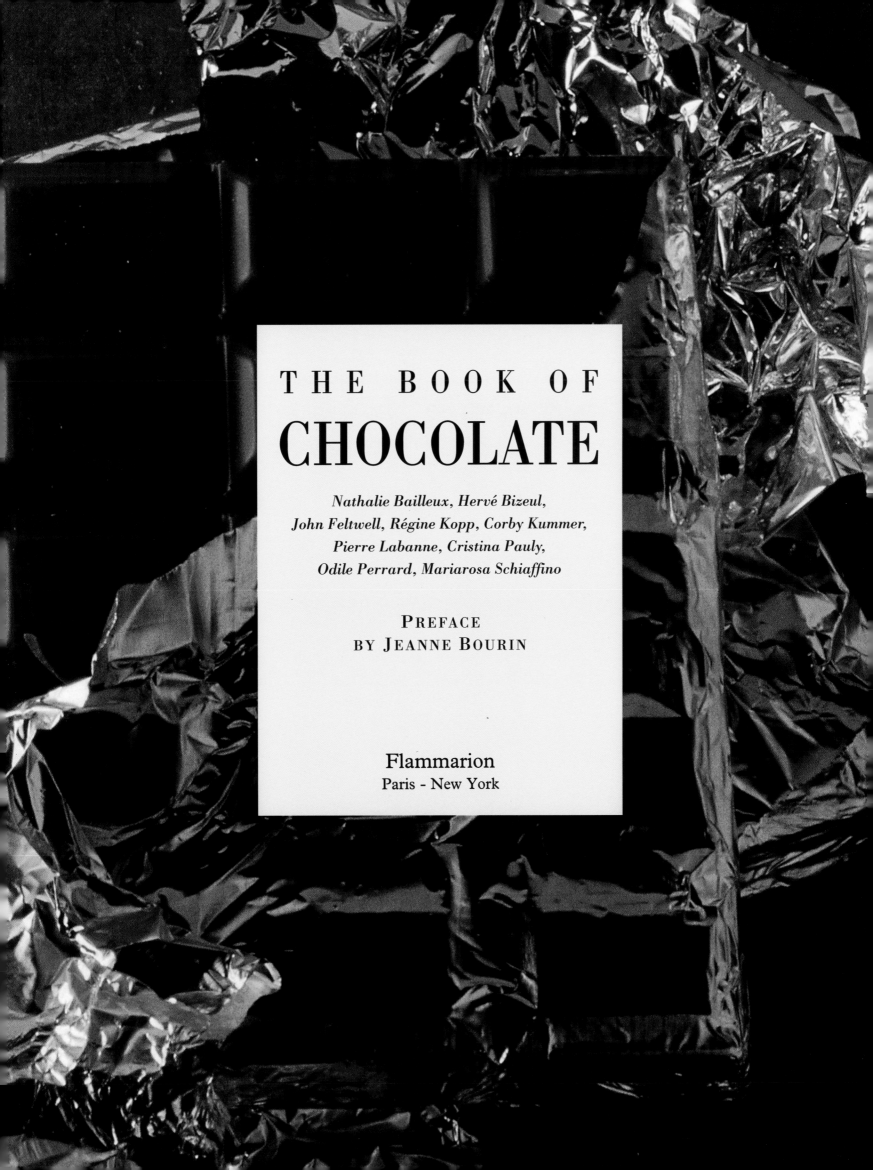

THE BOOK OF
CHOCOLATE

Nathalie Bailleux, Hervé Bizeul,
John Feltwell, Régine Kopp, Corby Kummer,
Pierre Labanne, Cristina Pauly,
Odile Perrard, Mariarosa Schiaffino

PREFACE
BY JEANNE BOURIN

Flammarion
Paris - New York

Originally published
in French as *Le Livre
du Chocolat*
© Flammarion, 1995

English-language edition
first published in 2001
ISBN: 2-0801-3588-0
© Flammarion

This edition © Éditions
Flammarion, 2004

All rights reserved. No
part of this publication
may be reproduced in
any form or by any
means, electronic,
photocopy, information
retrieval system, or
otherwise, without
written permission from
Éditions Flammarion.
26, rue Racine
75006 Paris

www.editions.flammarion.com

04 05 06 4 3 2 1

FC0479-05-I
ISBN: 2-0803-0479-8
Dépôt légal: 01/2005

*For Anne, Sarah,
Margot, and Adèle*

Translated from the
French by Tamara
Blondel. The section
on U.S. and British
chocolate by Corby
Kummer was originally
written in English.

Copyediting
Bernard Wooding

Typesetting
Éditions de l'Après-Midi

Research
Fui Lee Luk

Color Separation
Colourscan France

Distributed in North
America by Rizzoli
International
Publications, Inc.

Printed in Italy by
Canale

CONTENTS

SWEET TEMPTATION

by Jeanne Bourin

One of my most powerful childhood memories is of the deliciously promising aroma of chocolate wafting through our apartment. In those days, the 1930s, my mother was "at home" to visitors on the first and the third Fridays of the winter months. According to this custom, a relic from the nineteenth century, ladies used to reserve a carefully chosen day, "their day," when relatives, acquaintances or close friends could visit during the course of these jealously kept afternoons. It must be remembered that in those days few women in polite society worked, since this was frowned on in such circles, and so they had a great deal of time on their hands.

For her "Fridays," my mother baked a considerable quantity of cakes. She was an accomplished cook and prided herself on her pastries, which were as delicious as they were economical. Among her greatest successes was a chocolate charlotte which was a pure delight. While she was preparing it—and this felicitous moment occurred frequently—the smell of the chocolate held many a promise for me. I have always been a food lover and the evocative aroma of the melted chocolate filled me with anticipatory pleasure, for I knew that mother's friends would not finish the charlotte and that my sister and I would be able to blissfully eat the remains of this impressive cake.

However, it seems to me that my particularly pronounced fondness for chocolate comes from further afield. We had an aunt, whom we called Tante Licette, who, unlike my mother, made no attempt at being economical. She considered that the best brands ensured the best quality, and bought only the finest products. She was in the habit of bringing my sister and me delicious, creamy chocolate croquettes which were no doubt made of milk chocolate, since they were intended for children. I still remember them fondly. Fine, light, and delicate, they melted in the mouth so easily that they disappeared in no time, bringing down maternal scolding and punishment, all to no effect as only the pleasure prevailed.

Another memorable delight was béhanzin. This fabulous cake, no doubt because of its high chocolate content, bore the name of the last king of Dahomey, whose sad fate it was to be deported to Algeria after his kingdom was conquered by our ancestors. That, however, is of no importance, and indeed when I was seven or eight years old I didn't give a fig for these historical details, whereas the béhanzin, on the contrary, afforded me untold pleasure.

Delightfully old-fashioned lithographs, shop signs of yesteryear, images mellowed by time . . . chocolate makers have always sought to vaunt the merits of their products through advertising. Chocolate may be a dark temptation, but it is above all a delightfully irresistible pleasure. This chocolate maker's sign dates from the end of the nineteenth century (page 1). The traditional bar of dark chocolate (pages 2 and 3). A turn-of-the-century illustration depicting a chocolate girl, by the German artist V.G. Sturm (page 4). A lady pouring hot chocolate into a saucer to cool it down (page 5). Suchard advertisements dating from 1898 and 1920 (facing page and right).

It was a square cake made up of a series of alternate layers of the finest chocolate butter cream and a light hazelnut paste. Covered in chocolate powder, it had the dark velvety appearance of a beautiful dark chestnut, fully doing justice to its name.

My father used to buy it in the rue du Laos, not far from our apartment building, in a pastry shop which no longer exists. The delectable occasions on which this treat was served were limited to special days such as birthdays. We were so partial to béhanzin that my sister and I used to ask our parents for permission to cut off thin slices, which we kept in tins on our bedside tables so that we could savor it little by little and make the pleasure last as long as possible. I remember that, after a while, these little nibbled, half-eaten, pieces of cake that had been kept for too long so disgusted Mother that, much to our dismay, she used to throw them away when we were not there.

For tea we usually had bread and butter sprinkled with grated chocolate. Our maternal grandmother, who lived in La Chartre-sur-le-Loir, made her own salted butter, which she sent us in large stone pots. It kept fresh for a long time and it was this butter which we spread on the bread, and coated with grated chocolate, or ate with the foil-wrapped bars of Menier chocolate that Mother sometimes gave us.

This taste, which I still have to this day, for the sweetness, strength and seductive power of chocolate, has sometimes also been a source of grief. My father, who in those days was a government inspector, frequently received beautiful boxes of sweets or truffles at Christmas or New Year from the companies he had inspected and which hoped to curry favor by sending him these gifts. Now, my father took a very strict line with regard to the professional code of honesty expected of civil servants. He therefore systematically refused to accept the slightest gift he felt would violate this moral rule, and inexorably returned every one of those beribboned packages he received and which tempted us so terribly. I do not know how many of them I had longingly fondled and contemplated, only to see them sent away! I sorely missed them and greedily conjured up in my mind's eye all those irretrievable delicacies!

Sometimes, during the Second World War, there was an unexpected distribution of chocolate coupons, to which, being over twenty years old, we were entitled. Those were real field days. As soon as we could, we went to a shop in our neighborhood on the Left Bank to purchase and sample our ration of chocolate creams and other chocolate flavored sweets. We then shared this delicious booty with our parents.

I remember one of my friends telling me on the way home from the shop that she could not resist devouring her

"As a child," wrote author Irène Frain, "I used to climb quietly onto a stool to steal the bars of chocolate hidden away at the back of the cupboard." For this novelist, as for numerous other unrepentant chocoholics, chocolate is indissolubly linked with childhood. A reward for a well-behaved child: an advertisement for the Swiss chocolate Sprüngli, showing, in the background, the factory in Zurich and the lake (above). All the nostalgia of a French childhood is evoked by images of bread and butter sprinkled with grated chocolate (facing page).

entire ration. I, on the contrary, sought to prolong the pleasure for as long as I could, just as I had previously done with the béhanzin. I therefore rationed myself (and my sister did the same) to one chocolate or sweet per day, which we decided to eat after lunch. When the appropriate time arrived, we officiated with a mixture of greed and respect, lending an almost religious aspect to the ceremony. By acting in this fashion we unwittingly rejoined the Aztecs across the centuries, for whom the brown cacao beans were sacred objects brought to earth from Paradise by their god Quetzalcoatl. In the Aztec tradition, the various stages in the cultivation of cacao gave rise to numerous sensual fertility rites. Needless to say we were quite unaware of these facts, but I have no doubt that because of our passion for chocolate we would have had no difficulty in understanding them.

Many years later I had the opportunity of seeing cacao trees with my own eyes in Trinidad, formerly a British colony. I went there with my husband and daughter to attend the wedding of our eldest son, who was marrying a local girl of Hindu origin and religion. During our pleasant stay we were able to visit several picturesque regions of the island. During one such excursion, we found ourselves in a shady, tropical forest where we discovered some small unpretentious trees growing under the protective branches of much taller ones. My daughter-in-law, who knew that I took a great interest in botany and was also aware of my love of chocolate, showed me the reddish cacao pods which grew straight out from the branches and trunk of the trees. She then briefly described

the manner of picking, treating and utilizing these strange fruits, whose seeds are so precious that the Aztecs, when their empire was at its zenith, used them as a form of currency.

I was enchanted with Trinidad, whose cacao beans are still among the best in the world, despite the fact that the tree has also been introduced into Africa, whose climate is naturally very propitious. However, as with wine, different regions bring out different qualities.

If I remember correctly, it was on my return from Trinidad that I decided to join the Club des Croqueurs de Chocolat, a chocolate lovers' club of which I have since become an active member. We meet every two months to abandon ourselves to our shared passion, tasting the most varied and delicious chocolate creations. A different theme is chosen for each reunion, varying from homemade or industrial chocolate to chocolate bars, from ices and cakes to assorted chocolates or truffles. We solemnly compare them and award them marks, with the winner receiving advertising space and a mention in the *Guide des Croqueurs de Chocolat*. But above all these reunions, and the sumptuous annual dinner culminating in the inevitable numerous chocolate desserts, provide us connoisseurs, passionately devoted to choice dark chocolate, with an excuse to see each other regularly.

These club reunions, however, are not the only occasions when I am able to enjoy good chocolate, as I am in the habit of working with the help of this wonderful stimulant. At around three o'clock in the afternoon, I settle myself at the desk in my office, a small room

Some chocolate lovers are also passionate label collectors (right). Others yield to the temptations of the real thing, born of the imagination of chocolate makers. This lavish cake, called a "Conquistador," the work of a chocolatier from Burgundy, is filled with an exquisite praline made of almonds, pistachios, hazelnuts and candied orange peel (facing page). The truffles, displayed here on traditional grain scales (following double page), were prepared by Robert Linxe, one of the finest Parisian chocolatiers.

lined with bookshelves over-looking the garden, with its lawn and tutelary plane tree.

I have the good fortune to be able to write for a living and I am well aware that to have my work published and read by others is a rare and almost miraculous privilege. I work with pleasure and, I admit, in a sort of constant state of jubilation. I do not experience anxiety when confronted by a blank page, but rather by a written one. Faced with a blank sheet of paper, everything is possible, including the inspiration to write a masterpiece, whereas when rereading yesterday's text and realizing that everything needs correcting or rewriting, that is when I find myself in the grip of devastating anxiety.

However, I am incapable of working non-stop from three o'clock in the afternoon to eight o'clock in the evening. I therefore decided that at around five o'clock I would grant myself a chocolate break. Knowing that my cherished bars of hard, dark chocolate contain iron and magnesium, I allow myself three or four pieces, as much for pleasure as for health reasons. While eating the dark chocolate I drink a tall glass of water, and then, with renewed energy, I take up the enchanting work that is my source of income, which consists of telling myself stories in which I become completely immersed and

which transport me to imaginary places and bygone days.

You will tell me, perhaps, that gastronomic indulgence is a sin. I quite agree, but what can I do about it? I came into this world with a relish for life and its gifts, and chocolate happens to be one of the most tempting that one can possibly imagine.

Moreover, is it not our fate in this world to wrestle incessantly, endlessly, with temptation? When it is not gluttony that torments me, it is the vanity which incites me to diet in order to lose the surplus pounds brought on by my first indulgence. Torn between the desire to give myself up to the temptation of chocolate and that of losing weight, I experience ups and downs in which rigor and gustatory pleasures alternate. However, I must admit that as the years pass rigor seems to me to be increasingly distasteful and also, in the long run, pointless.

Well, it cannot be helped! A gourmand I was born and a gourmand I will remain—a gourmand with a very strong predilection for that good, hard, dark chocolate. If it is a sin, may God forgive me. But, as a clergyman friend of ours was fond of saying, weren't good things created so that we might benefit from them, and if so, wouldn't it be an even graver sin to scorn them?

Hot chocolate, a delicious beverage which has remained popular down the centuries, has become the symbol of a certain gracious lifestyle. As a tribute to Edith Sitwell's superior taste, photographer Cecil Beaton portrayed her, bejeweled and turbaned, reclining on her bed in her house in Renishaw, Derbyshire, receiving her morning cup of chocolate (facing page). Two elegant society women "taking" their chocolate at the turn of the century (above).

· CACAO ·
PLANTATIONS

In the depths of the Amazonian forest it is no easy task to clear a path through the labyrinth of damp, stifling greenery. The air is saturated with humidity, making breathing laborious. Iridescent butterflies flutter among the branches and a multitude of vividly colored birds dance in the sunlight. High above, a patch of blue sky is visible between the treetops. Far below, in the depths of the gloom, cacao trees have grown in the shade of the taller trees. Their bark is very fine and has silver patches. Their straight trunks are slender and smooth, extending gracefully upwards to disappear in the canopy of thick foliage. Their crowns of interlaced branches look like strange headdresses. The dark green oblong leaves of the cacao trees glisten in the half-light; their small white and pink flowers blossom in dense clusters. Cacao trees bear large fruits, called pods, which contain the precious cacao seeds, or beans. The term cacao, essentially a botanical name, refers to the tree, the pods, and the seeds, as well as to the fermented beans in bulk. Cacao pods have no stems, sprouting straight out from the trunk, and they grow to various sizes. Young pods are identified by their green or reddish violet color, but by the time they are ripe and ready to be picked, they have turned yellow or orange.

Heat, humidity and shade—the same conditions prevail in plantations all over the world. The cacao tree is delicate and can only thrive if protected from direct sunlight in a hot, damp climate not subject to significant temperature variations. It is cultivated in the tropics in a band which extends 20 degrees above and below the equator, with Cuba at the northernmost latitude and the island of Réunion at the southern limit. Cacao trees grow in semidarkness in the shade of tall trees, preferably at an altitude of between 1,300 and 2,300 feet.

All cacao trees need shade in order to thrive. Almost all the oldest plantations in the world were cultivated in existing forests. For long months, the planters battled with nature in order to clear plots of land in the heart of

VIEW OF COCOA WALK AND DRYING HOUSE, TRINIDAD.

The legendary Chuao plantation, hidden in the mountains of Venezuela, is one of the most famous in the world. The fine, delicate cocoa produced from these beans is the dream of all chocolate lovers. To reach it one has to cross the tropical forest (facing page). At the end of the last century, reputable brands of chocolate possessed their own plantations (above: the plantation belonging to J.S. Fry & Sons in Trinidad, in the 1870s). An important moment on the plantation: harvesting the fruit of cacao trees in Cameroon (page 16). A sack of freshly harvested and dried cacao beans (page 17).

tropical forests. The great epoch of the conquest of the forests in the south of the Brazilian state of Bahia is brought to life in the work of Brazilian novelist Jorge Amado, who was born on a plantation. In one of several novels based on life on the plantations, Amado wrote of the men's fear of the mysterious jungle, men who had "come from other lands, other seas and other forests, forests conquered by man, with roads and clearings obtained by burning the vegetation, forests from which the jaguars had disappeared and where snakes were rare."

Amado tells of cacao fever and the planter's determination: "He too was face to face with the forest, he too saw the lightning and heard the thunder rumble, the growling of the jaguar and the hiss of the snake, he too felt his heart miss a beat on hearing the eerie cry of the owl."

But this man's eyes saw a different vision: "He does not see the forest illuminated by lightning, bristling with strange sounds, choked with dense creepers and century-old trees, inhabited by wild animals and apparitions. He sees fields planted with cacao trees, straight rows of trees bearing golden fruit, ripe and yellow. He sees plantations pushing the forest back and stretching as far as the horizon."

The techniques used are ancestral and the air resounds with the impact of machete and axe on timber. Tall trees are generally spared to permit the cacao trees to grow in their shade. Plantations are buried deep in the jungle, hemmed in by its dense foliage. They are never very extensive: a few acres at most, sometimes even less than two acres. Today, some plantations are increasing in size, a trend

The best and oldest plantations, which produce the delicate beans sought after by chocolate makers all over the world, are located in South and Central America. Above: the island of Grenada, one of the bastions of Caribbean cacao bean production; facing page: the Clementina plantation in Ecuador, one of the first countries to cultivate cacao.

which is encouraged in many countries by both state-owned and private development companies. On the whole, however, large cacao plantations are still the exception.

When plantations are not situated in a forest, fast-growing umbrella trees are planted at the same time as cacao saplings. Wide-leafed banana trees, coconut, mango, palm or lemon trees are used, or a *Gliricidia sepium*, a very tall tree originally from the tropical forests of Central and South America, whose cascades of rose-colored blossoms brighten plantations all over the world. Planters call this tree the *madre del cacao*, the "cacao mother." The *Erythrina*, or coral tree, characterized by voluminous, rapidly growing foliage, may also be used as a sun shield, as are yellow-flowering acacias.

On some modern plantations, planters have succeeded in growing cacao trees in direct sunlight without any protection whatsoever. This is the case, for example, in Hawaii, where planter Jim Walsh harvests the only cacao beans cultivated in the United States, which are used to make Hawaiian Vintage Chocolate. It is also the case in South America. When the French chocolatier Christian Constant paid a visit to a plantation there, he was surprised to see cacao saplings growing in full sunlight. "A treatment of fertilizer and hormones is used," he explains, "resulting in the rapid development of dense foliage which provides the

necessary shade." Although these experiments are becoming more frequent nowadays, they are nevertheless the exception and cacao remains a fruit of the shade.

In its native region in the tropical Amazonian forest, the cacao tree grows wild at the foot of giant trees. The rainfall is between 70 and 90 inches and the temperature always between 70 and 85°F. Gradually the "chocolate tree" has captured the imagination of the entire world. The first to cultivate it were the Maya and the Aztecs in what is now Mexico. In the sixteenth century, at the instigation of the Spaniards, cacao cultivation was developed in Central and South America, in Mexico, Venezuela, and Ecuador. Over the centuries it spread further across the continent of South America, especially to Brazil, as well as to the Caribbean islands of Trinidad, Hispaniola (the first European name of the island now shared by Haiti and the Dominican Republic), Martinique, and Jamaica. Today, the noblest varieties are still found in these regions.

In the nineteenth century, the Portuguese planted Brazilian saplings on the island of São Tomé off the African coast. Cultivation was subsequently developed on the island of Bioko (formerly Fernando Poo) and from there, at the end of the century, it spread to West Africa, the present-day Ivory Coast, Nigeria, and Cameroon.

As for the Dutch, they transported the tree to Java and Sumatra at the beginning

A majestic cathedral of foliage, the tropical forest is like an enchanted kingdom to the traveler, abounding in trees bearing extraordinary fruit and flowers, multicolored birds, and magnificent butterflies fluttering in the sunlight. It is here, in the protective shade of massive jungle trees, that the precious cacao tree grows, the tree of the Maya and the Aztecs (facing page). In plantations all over the world, the delicate, fragile cacao tree is generally cultivated in the shade of flower-bearing trees whose blossoms bathe the landscape in color (above: *Gliricidia sepium*).

of the seventeenth century and from there it gradually spread to Sri Lanka, New Guinea, Samoa, Indonesia, the former New Hebrides, and the Philippines.

Since then the cultivation of cacao has extended still further. The countries of Southeast Asia, Malaysia in particular, have developed plantations where new methods of cacao cultivation and bean processing are being developed. "Perhaps they will be as successful as hevea trees, which also originated in South America," suggests chocolatier Christian Constant.

Today the Ivory Coast, Brazil, and Malaysia are the leading producers. They supply almost 50 percent of the two million tons of beans sold annually throughout the world. However, although South and Central America have now lost their supremacy, they nevertheless possess the best plantations, those which provide the finest cacao beans, the criollos and trinitarios so highly prized by chocolate manufacturers all over the world. Cacao was born in the New World and has never forgotten its origins.

This German planter and his wife (above), posing by a cacao tree in Samoa at the beginning of the century, could well be characters out of a novel by Robert Louis Stevenson, who spent the last years of his life in Samoa. Stevenson wrote about the plantations of the South Pacific, which had become a veritable El Dorado for Europeans. Formerly, when harvesting was over, a dance was performed on the cacao seeds which had been put out to dry in the sun. This tradition, which consists of dancing barefoot on the beans to make them shine, continues today in certain regions of Central and South America (facing page: beans drying on the rooftops on a plantation in Trinidad).

THE CHOCOLATE TREE

All cacao trees belong to the *Theobroma* genus, literally "drink of the gods" (from the Greek *theos* meaning "god" and *broma*, "beverage"). Swedish naturalist Carolus Linnaeus so named the tree in the eighteenth century as a tribute to the beverage of the Maya and Aztecs. He knew of only one variety. Today botanists have been able to identify a number of different varieties, of which three main types are cultivated for cacao production: criollo, forastero, and trinitario.

Criollo (meaning "indigenous") was the name originally given by the Spanish to the cacao tree cultivated by the Indians. It had been the "chocolate tree" of the Maya and was the legendary variety cultivated by the Aztec god Quetzalcoatl, the mythical gardener of Paradise. The Spanish were the first to bring the criollo beans to Europe, where the variety was also known as *caraque*. The criollo tree produces the finest cacao beans, very aromatic with a slightly bitter and yet delicate flavor. Chocolate manufacturers always use these beans in combination with other varieties. The trees are extremely delicate, with low yields, and their cultivation requires meticulous care. Today this exceptional cacao bean is only produced on a very small scale and accounts for not more than 5 to 10 percent of world production. It is mainly cultivated in the Central and South American countries where cacao originated, namely Venezuela, Mexico, Nicaragua, Guatemala, and Colombia, as well as Trinidad, Grenada, and Jamaica.

Next comes the group known as forastero (meaning "foreign" in Spanish) originally from the upper Amazon. These varieties produce the majority of the African cacao crop. Forastero trees were introduced on the island of São Tomé during the colonial era and cultivation gradually spread to the western side of Africa. Forastero varieties are also cultivated in Brazil, the West Indies, Central America and, to an increasing extent, in South America. The trees grow faster and are much hardier than criollo trees, and they also produce more fruit, accounting for nearly 80 percent of world production. The forastero, which is the most widely used type of bean, has a strong, bitter flavor and an acid aroma. It is frequently used in blends. There is, however, one exception: the amenolado variety of forastero. This variety produces the delicate, aromatic "Nacional" (or "Arriba") bean, which is cultivated in Ecuador and is comparable to the world's finest.

Finally, there are the trinitarios, which are crossbreeds between criollos and forasteros. Their history began off the coast of Venezuela, in Trinidad, the island from which they take their name. The soil, climate, and traditions of this Caribbean island, where Spanish colonists planted criollo trees, have

Work never stops on the plantations. From dawn to dusk the trees have to be treated, pruned, looked after, and protected from insects, which would otherwise devour the leaves, flowers, pods, and seeds. Any damage done to the cacao trees would affect the flavor of the future cocoa, so the workers are always extremely careful, especially when handling machetes, one of their principal tools (above, on a plantation in Colombia).

transformed it, over the centuries, into a great "land of chocolate." At the beginning of the eighteenth century, a hurricane destroyed the plantations. The islanders then planted forasteros from the Orinoco valley. Meanwhile, some criollos had survived, and the new group of varieties was born from natural intercrossings which grew easily and proved to be far hardier. Trinitarios produce fine cacao beans with a high fat content, and represent 10 to 15 percent of world production. They are mainly cultivated in Central and South America, Indonesia and Sri Lanka. The quality, however, varies depending on the region. The best trinitario cacaos are indisputably those grown on their native island.

Guayaquil cacao beans are sweet, beans from Madagascar are strong, those grown in Sri Lanka are slightly acid, while Samoa produces aromatic beans. As with wine, each regional soil produces beans with a specific aroma and more or less marked characteristics. For example, cacao beans from Ecuador are highly scented, whereas the Brazilian variety is reputed to have a smoky taste. Grand cru chocolates are made from one single variety of bean. The remainder, the vast majority, are composed of subtle blends, which combine the strength of certain beans with the aroma of other carefully chosen varieties.

In his guide to commercial natural products entitled *Les Produits naturels commerçables*, published in Paris in

1892, Émile Dubois drew up an inventory of the best cacao varieties of the period. He used the term caraque instead of criollo, but, apart from this etymological detail, his list is still perfectly valid.

First of all he listed "Venezuelan cacaos, the most highly prized and expensive variety, with their colorful names: caraques from Chuao Chouni, Ocumare and San Felipe, as large as olives and of a beautiful reddish gray color; the long, thick, gray-brown beans of the Maracaibo cacaos; the fine, almond-shaped Carupana cacaos, etc." Then come "Trinidad cacaos with their flat beans," and "Ecuador cacaos (guayaquil, carriba, balao malacha, etc.), whose long, wide, flat beans are slightly less fine and brown in color." Next on the list are "Brazilian cacaos (maragnan, para, and bahia), considered mediocre if used alone, but ideal for blends due to their robustness," followed by "Cayenne cacaos whose bitter almonds are rich in butter." Finally, "Martinique cacaos with their slate-gray flesh, wine-flavored Bourbon cacaos, Sinnamary cacaos with their acrid taste and smoky smell, etc."

Today, the chocolate maker's palette is neither less exotic nor less varied. This is confirmed by the range of cacao beans Robert Linxe describes in his *La Maison du chocolat*: "Among the varieties which attract me most is the Madagascar, which has a very strong and slightly acrid taste. One's palate is literally

Africa embarked on the cacao adventure in the nineteenth century and is now the world's leading producer. The president of the Ivory Coast, Félix Houphouët-Boigny, himself a planter's son, has encouraged the development of plantations. Thanks to the quality of its cacao beans and to the president's support, the Ivory Coast has become one of the most prestigious cacao-producing countries (above).

overwhelmed by it. . . . On the other hand, the Indian Ocean cacaos, from Ceylon and Indonesia, for example . . . are slightly pungent and sourish, but not bitter. They are very aromatic, quite superb when the paste is first tasted, but afterwards nothing remains. They have to be blended with other, more robust varieties. The Caribbean cacao is round, soft and aromatic. The slightly acrid arriba variety from Trinidad is wonderful for blending. . . . Cacao from Sumatra is the most acid of all. It comes from damp, sunny mountainous regions. Finally, African cacao is cultivated in Ghana and Togo and nearly every country on the African continent, but above all in the Ivory Coast, which accounts for 70 percent of the African cacao bean production. Once they have been well cleaned, dried and fermented, they give a good chocolate flavor, somewhat aggressive and hard-hitting, but clear and strong."

As with wine, chocolate also has its grands crus, and certain plantations have a reputation comparable to those of the great French wine-producing châteaux. Chuao, in Venezuela, is one of these mythical places. It produces a legendary cacao bean, whose name has always been the stuff of connoisseurs' dreams. This bean has a fine, delicate aroma, and is all the rarer since it is now impossible to procure beans exclusively from this plantation because they are blended with other varieties from the region before arriving on the market.

This plantation was created in the seventeenth century in a wild, isolated region on the coast near Caracas, at the base of a steep mountain range which drops sharply into the Caribbean. The only access is by sea and for an hour the boat follows the wild coastline as

far as the Chuao creek. As it glides slowly towards the shore, the landing stage, the boats which transport the beans, and a sprinkling of wooden houses can be made out. Dry land at last. Chocolatier Christian Constant, in his book on chocolate, describes this enchanted moment. "I penetrate the forest, under the canopy of tropical trees, where the air is still just as humid—tall mango trees with their serrated foliage, immense bamboo groves as high as buildings, plantains and breadfruit trees. . . . From time to time, a cacao tree with purplish red fruit grows beside a path punctuated by irrigation canals. The vegetation becomes denser and, not far from the sugar canes, a great many other cacao trees come into view. As regards the variety cultivated, this plantation appears to be very homogenous. A patch of sky, two paths bordered by habitations made of earth and bamboo, and the freshly painted church behind the cement square where the cacao beans are drying . . . Nothing has changed for centuries."

In Chuao and on plantations throughout the world, the scene is identical. Men move slowly between the cacao trees where the forest once grew. Day after day, they prune the trees, preventing the top branches from getting entangled and training them to form a high canopy of foliage to protect the fruit. They constantly weed the ground, straighten the branches, and cut off the broken ones. The quality of the future chocolate depends on this meticulous care.

The first rays of sunlight beat down on the blossoming cacao trees. In the wild they can grow up to 33 feet high. On plantations they are pruned down to a height of 16 to 20 feet

"I picked these yellow fruits resembling small cucumbers, in which the red seeds nestle," wrote James de Coquet in his *Propos de table*. "They are acrid and bitter. One has to have tasted them to be able to measure the full extent of man's genius for satisfying his appetite for voluptuous pleasure." After drying in the sun for about ten days, the seeds turn into beautiful coffee-colored beans which already harbor all the riches of the future chocolate.

so that the cacao pods are easier to reach. Pruning also forces the trees to grow widthwise, thereby creating their own shade. Their branches are trained to meet and form a perfect roof, which protects the fruit from the sun and enables the men to move around with ease on the plantation.

Buds emerge from the bark, and the flowers appear at the beginning of the rainy season in America and Africa, if there is one, and all the year round in regions where there are no seasons, such as Malaysia, for example. The blooms, which barely last a day, bathe the plantation in color.

The fruit—the cacao pod—develops from a fertilized flower. Although the tree bears thousands of flowers a year, only one in a hundred is destined to reach this state. On some plantations, pollination occurs naturally through the good offices of small insects. Other cacao tree groves rely on the dexterity of young girls, who deftly accomplish this work with a fine brush. The cacao pods, growing straight out of the trunk, turn golden in the sun. It

seems impossible that this fruit could come from such a small delicate flower. In fact the flowering cycle is uninterrupted, so pods in all stages of development grow among the flowers. One can see flowers with pale pink stamens next to purplish red pods, which, in the case of criollo varieties, are pointed at one end. The forastero trees produce flowers with violet stamens among green or yellow pods, either elongated or rounded, while those of the trinitario varieties vary in color.

Cacao pods are very hard and have an elongated, more or less pointed shape. Some resemble a small rugby ball, others a cucumber or a large gourd. It takes five to seven months for them to reach their full size, which can be as much as 10 inches. The precious almond-shaped cacao seeds (an average of thirty to forty per pod) are concealed inside. They are embedded in a bittersweet pulp, which in former times is said to have been the delight of the Creole ladies. As for the Maya, it is known that for many years they made no use of the beans, but were also very partial to

The fruits of the cacao tree, which take the form of heavy pods, are very colorful. They go from bright red through various subtle intermediary tones to lemon yellow. Ripeness is judged by their color or by the rattling of seeds when the pods are shaken. A European buyer makes his selection from pods still growing on the trees in the Chuao plantation in Venezuela (above).

the sharp, slightly sweet pulp. The best beans, the criollos, are rounded and can be recognized by their white, almost translucent appearance. The forasteros are flat and of a deep purple color, whereas the trinitarios vary depending on the variety.

The productivity of a cacao tree depends largely on the plantation, the variety, the age of the tree, the care with which it is tended, and the quality of the soil. In South America, a tree yields on average thirty to thirty-five pods, compared to only about twenty in Africa. A well-tended cacao tree lives for approximately fifty to sixty years, but in certain very old plantations, particularly in Brazil, it is sometimes possible to come across quite "elderly" trees of more than eighty years of age.

Early explorers have left numerous descriptions of the cultivation of this delicate tree. In his account of his experiences in Mexico in the late seventeenth century, the Italian explorer, Giovanni Francesco Gemelli Careri, described in great detail the methods employed by the planters of New Spain: "The cacao seeds are planted with the eye uppermost, well down in warm, damp soil. They emerge at the end of a fortnight, and within two years grow to a height of three palms. They are then dug up with the clod of earth protecting the roots and planted with support stakes in rows eighteen palms apart. Plantains (that is to say banana plants) or other fruit trees are planted around them to provide the necessary shade for the cacao trees to thrive. New shoots, which would hinder the tree's development, have to be removed and the ground well weeded. In addition, care has to be taken that the saplings do not suffer from the cold, excessive rain, and from certain worms. At the end of five years, the trees have grown thick, measure around seven palms, and begin to bear fruit. The leaves are similar to those of chestnut trees, but slightly narrower; flowers sprout all over the trunk and branches in much the same way as jasmine, but scarcely a quarter of them survive. A small spike, like that of Indian corn, emerges from the flower. At the outset, it is of greenish color. When ripe, it turns to chestnut

On the garden island of Grenada, with its torrents and mountains, excellent cacao trees are cultivated. The beans are appreciated by connoisseurs the world over. In the shady nursery of one of the island's plantations, young plants are tended with extreme care (above). The precious cacao seeds are concealed inside the pods and embedded in a white pulp, which the Maya regarded as a delicacy (following double page).

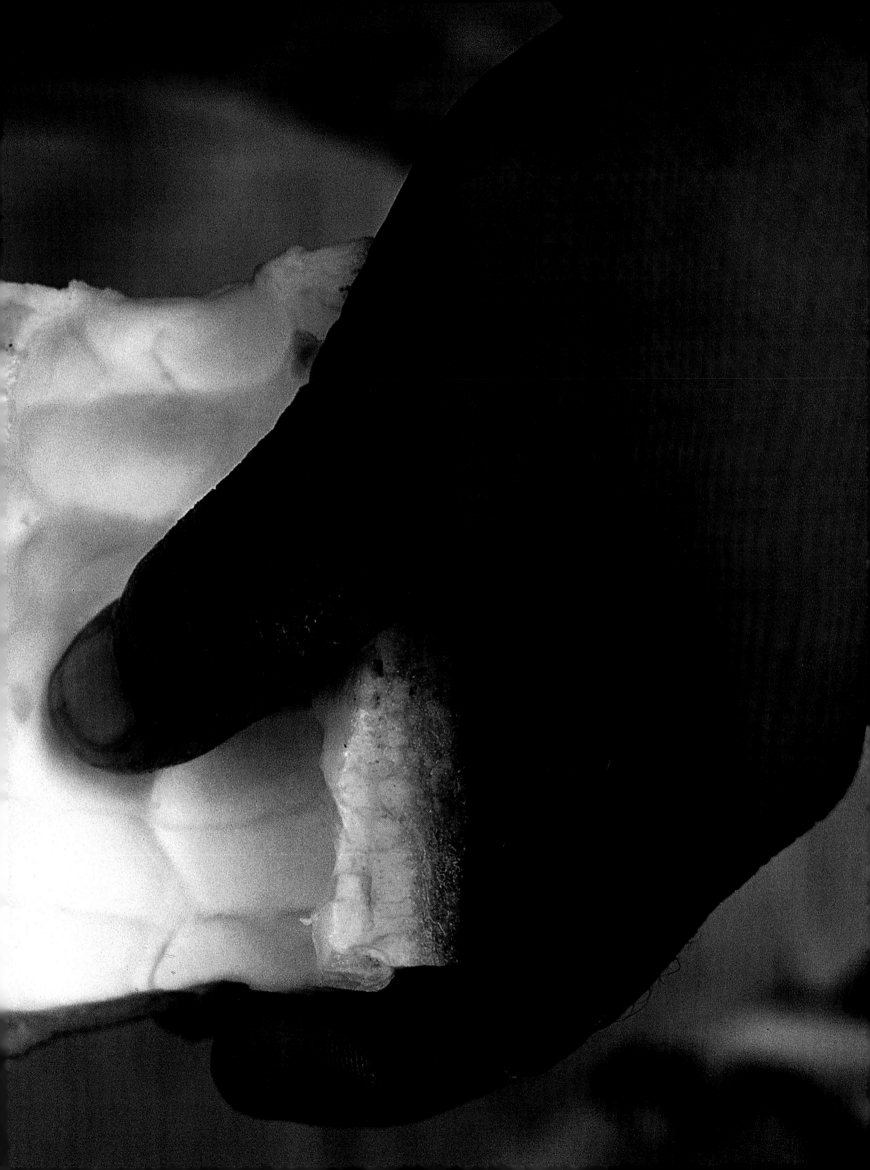

brown, or sometimes yellow, white and blue. These spikes contain ten or fifteen downy cacao seeds."

This description is still relevant today. Nowadays on plantations, everything begins in the nursery, where the shade is denser. The young plants are shielded by the foliage of specially planted shade trees or tall forest trees. On more recent plantations, the saplings are sometimes protected from the sun by artificial screens, but this is where nurseries tend to lose some of their poetry and charm.

In pre-Columbian times, the Aztecs were careful to ensure the goodwill of their god Quetzalcoatl. "To obtain the cacao bean," recounts Michel Onfray in *La Maison gourmande*, "Dionysian rituals had to be observed, involving the sacrifice of rust-colored dogs (the color of cacao mixtures), orgiastic dances, propitiatory rites, and masked frenzies." Today cacao trees no longer require these measures, but there are a number of techniques involved in growing new trees. On some plantations, workers enclose the cacao seeds in little sacks of earth, and within five days the heat and humidity cause them to germinate. Elsewhere, they carefully remove a root or a branch from a cacao tree and carefully replant it. From this cutting an identical new tree will grow.

After a few weeks, the saplings proudly raise their heads. The workers tend the "babies" with all the attention of young mothers. In these tropical climates, parasites and fungi develop very rapidly, and viruses and diseases are a real bane. Furthermore, the trees have to be protected from insects which devour the leaves, flowers, pods, and seeds.

The criollo varieties of cacao tree, which produce the highest quality beans, are only grown in the countries where the cacao tree originated, in Central and South America and the Caribbean islands. These delicate trees require meticulous care, without which the quality of the future chocolate would suffer (above, weeding in an area of young cacao trees in Colombia).

The workers, carrying sacks of pesticide and insecticide on their backs, cover with a fine spray all the trees in the nursery and on the plantation. Generally these products are neutralized as soon as they touch the ground. Without this treatment, these fragile trees would fall prey to serious diseases which would alter the flavor of the beans.

For centuries, plantation workers have carried out the same routine tasks. The days are punctuated by the regular watering sessions. The forest is alive with bird song. In the sun, the heat is almost unbearable, but in the nursery the air is almost cool. The saplings are closely lined up on the ground or on bamboo trestles. After a few months, they are bedded out under a shade tree. They flower two or three years later, but only bear their first fruit when three or four years old.

Jorge Amado captured the magic of dawn breaking on the plantations. "Drops of sunlight fall between the cacao tree branches. They break into rays on the ground and are reflected in the puddles which take on a tea rose hue. They are like topazes showering down from the sky which change into tea rose petals when landing on the scorched, dusty ground. All shades of yellow can be seen in the peaceful mornings on the cacao plantations. When a light breeze blows, the whole of this yellow sea undulates, the tints mingle and create a new yellow, the yellow of the cacao plantations. Oh it is the most beautiful yellow in the world, as only the *Grapiunas* are able to see it in the low season. There are no words to describe it, no images with which to compare it. It is an incomparable yellow, it is the yellow of the cacao plantations!"

The first cacao tree in Ghana is said to have been planted in 1898 in the village of Mapong. Today, this West African country has become one of the world's leading producers. Here, cacao trees are cultivated on small plantations, which are often family enterprises. Guardians of the tradition, these village chiefs, solemnly gathered together under the Mapong cacao trees, are all cacao planters.

FROM THE POD TO THE BEAN

Harvesting the cacao pods is a high point of life on the plantation. Jorge Amado, himself the son of a planter, knows better than anyone the history of these lands where the cacao trees grow. In his first novel, *Cacao*, he recounts the long days a young worker, Sergipano, spent on a large Brazilian cacao plantation in the early 1930s. "There were a great many of us working on the immense plantation. The dry leaves of the cacao plant carpet the earth where snakes warmed themselves in the sun after the long rains of June. The fruits hang from the trees like old lamps. The marvelous mixture of colors makes everything beautiful and unreal, except our exhausting work. By seven in the morning we were already removing the beans from the pods, after sharpening our machetes in front of the shop. Earlier, at five o'clock a glass of firewater and a plate of beans had fortified us for the day's work."

Since those days, nothing has really changed. Although the trees bear fruit all year round, rain accelerates flowering, and harvesting is generally concentrated in two main periods during the year, at the end of the first rainy season and at the beginning of the second wherever there is one. In regions with heavy rainfall and no marked dry season, such as in Malaysia, there are no significant peak seasons and the pods are picked all the year round as soon as they are ripe enough.

It is important for the cacao pods to reach complete maturity, otherwise the seeds dry badly and have a disagreeably bitter flavor. It is usually possible to tell whether they are ripe by their color. They turn from purplish red to orange and from green to yellow, but these guidelines cannot be used as general rules. On this subject, chocolatier Christian Constant explains that in Surinam, where the pods are almost always purplish in color, pickers identify the ripe fruit by ear. The pods should make a dull sound when tapped lightly with the fingers, and the seeds should be distinctly heard rattling against each other.

Pickers never climb cacao trees because the plants are extremely fragile and any injury to them affects the flavor of the future chocolate. Plantation workers are always careful never to damage the trees in any way. As dawn breaks, the pickers advance in small groups among the cacao trees. They carry long poles with a sharp knife or sickle at one end. When they locate ripe pods, they delicately remove them without touching the tree or damaging the flowers or unripe pods. The pods that are within easy reach are removed by hand, the others by means of the pole. The women in their colorful garments follow the men; they are sleek-haired Indians, Africans draped in shimmering fabrics, or almond-eyed Asians, depending on the plantation. They pile up the pods, transfer them to large

Since colonial times the harvest ritual has hardly changed. To remove the pods, the pickers usually use a pole fitted with a sharp blade which enables them to reach the highest fruit (above, harvest time in Cameroon; facing page, freshly picked pods).

baskets and carry them away on their heads.

In Brazil, where cacao is mainly cultivated in the northeastern state of Bahia, many workers have slave ancestors. "We went out in the mornings," recounts Jorge Amado, "with the long poles which had small sickles on the ends of them, gleaming in the sun . . . Me, Honorio, Nilo, Valentin, and some six others were gathering. Magnolia, Old Julia, Simeon, Rita, Joao Grilo and others collected and opened the pods. What remained were heaps of white pulp from which the honey trickled away. We pickers were separated from each other and could scarcely exchange a world. On the other hand, the ones who were collecting them into piles talked and laughed. . . . At noon (the sun served as our clock), we stopped work and joined the collecting team for the midday meal. We ate the piece of dried meat and the black beans that had been cooked in the morning and passed around a bottle of tafia. We clicked our tongues and spat a good deal. We talked and took no notice of the snakes which glided by making strange noises in the dry leaves covering the ground."

The picking continues. The men sing ancient melodies, their voices trailing off into the depths of the plantation. The cacao pods fall with a dull thud, and are not kept waiting long. On the plantations of Brazil, as elsewhere, they are opened immediately after picking or even during picking. The pod-split-

ting operation takes place on site, in the shade of the cacao trees. The men and women who are given this task split the pods diagonally with a sharp knife or a machete. It is a delicate operation which requires a great deal of skill, for if the outer shell of the seed is damaged, it will be vulnerable to attacks by insects and fungi. Sometimes the huskers prefer opening the pods by striking them on a stone or hitting them with a log. The gestures, unerring and rapid, have remained unchanged since time immemorial.

The cacao pods offer no resistance and when opened reveal seeds coated with a white, sticky pulp which is both acidic and slightly sweet. The pod-splitters scoop the seeds out by hand and pile them up in baskets, sacks or buckets. On some modern plantations, automatic podding machines are used. This means the pods have to be transported to the machine, which, because of their weight, is a tedious task. Consequently, as often as not the pods are emptied by hand. Twenty fresh pods yield an average of 2 to 2½ pounds of dried cacao beans.

The open pods gradually pile up at the pod-splitters' feet. In Nigeria, the pods are collected, ground into powder and used for making wine, brandy or cacao vinegar. Elsewhere they are used as fertilizer or animal feed. In most cases, however, they are simply left under the cacao trees, making the pod-splitting areas on plantations easy to identify.

The Aztecs used to prepare an astonishing "drink of the gods," a mixture consisting of a ground cacao bean base enriched with spices and corn. This Mexican woman (above) has prepared her paste according to a local recipe, no doubt very similar to that of her ancient predecessors. An important moment on the plantation: opening the freshly harvested pods under the cacao trees. The cacao beans are scooped out by hand and gradually piled up in large baskets. One man can open as many as two thousand pods a day (facing page: a plantation in Trinidad).

At this stage, the soft, spongy seeds, which are prettily veined and flecked with delicate pink tones, do not taste of chocolate at all. Anyone curious enough to taste one would find it to be slightly acrid and very bitter. The pulp has to be removed as quickly as possible. It could simply be rinsed off, but this would transform the flavor and spoil the cacao's future aroma. Over the years a technique known as "fermentation" has been developed.

Fermentation determines the flavor of the future chocolate. The more rapid the process, the better the cacao. The object is to turn the seed into a bean by means of a combination of chemical transformations. This operation destroys the seed's embryo thus preventing germination, but above all it produces the cacao's aroma, or, more precisely, it provokes the development of the precursors of the aroma.

This somewhat magical and mysterious process is true alchemy, which scientists are able to explain only with the aid of a considerable amount of technical detail. The fact is that almost five hundred substances can be identified in a single seed, all of which contribute to chocolate's particular flavor. These substances include cocoa butter, albumin, starch, theobromine (a nerve stimulant), and coloring substances. Some are responsible for the specific brown color of cacao, others are the famous aroma precursors, without which cocoa would be tasteless.

On large plantations, the fermentation process is generally centralized and takes place in long, low buildings in large clearings in the tropical forest. Sometimes these places can only be reached after long hours of walking. On the vast Brazilian plantations, one sometimes comes across convoys of mules transporting large baskets of seeds.

The seeds are piled up on large banana leaves spread out on the ground and covered with more leaves. Then the longest part of the process begins: the waiting. The length of the

In Ghana, the photographer Marc Riboud was impressed by the beauty of the gestures used in the processing of cacao seeds. His camera has captured their ancestral movements, repeated since time immemorial, the meticulous fan-shaped arrangement of the leaves on the ground, and the colorful heaps of seeds. The empty baskets lie abandoned in the sun. Behind them, beans dry on imposing elevated grids. Here, nothing has changed since the time of the first planters (facing page and above).

operation depends on the variety. The criollos need only two or three days, whereas the forasteros and the trinitarios require a week or more. The duration, which is carefully calculated, determines the quality of the beans. Too short or too lengthy a fermentation would have an adverse affect on the flavor of the chocolate which is eventually produced. The duration may also be determined in accordance with consumer tastes. The French, for example, prefer cocoa with a well-developed aroma which necessitates prolonged fermentation, whereas the English-speaking world generally prefers blander cocoa obtained by rapid fermentation.

In the heat, the pulp covering the seeds melts and drains off. Sometimes this juice is collected for making jam, jelly, or confectionery. Plantation workers regularly turn the piles of seeds over to air them and ensure even fermentation. The seeds change color; the criollos turn brownish yellow and the forasteros end up slightly darker, almost violet-colored. The seeds, which prior to this phase were bitter, are now sweet.

The various techniques employed throughout the world are all based on this principle. In Nigeria, the seeds are fermented in baskets covered with leaves. In the Ivory Coast, they are placed on large trays piled one on top of the other. Elsewhere, the seeds are buried in a hole and covered with leaves. In South America and the West Indies, large, latticed, wooden fermentation crates are used, each of which

The island of São Tomé in the Gulf of Guinea, a former Portuguese colony, was the first cacao region to be developed in Africa. Here the beans are still dried in the sun according to the traditional methods imported from South America (above and facing page). In the Chuao Valley, in Venezuela, the cacao bean is still cultivated just as it was at the time of the Aztecs. On this remote plantation, founded in the seventeenth century, several tons of seeds are harvested annually. Fermentation takes place under banana leaves, and later the beans are dried in the sun in front of the church. The plantation produces the rarest and finest cacao beans (following double page).

can contain about 150 pounds of seeds. The crates are placed in a large, airy, but windowless room. The seeds are regularly tipped from one crate to another to air them. In Southeast Asia, a sophisticated process based on the same principle is used. Large crates are fixed one on top of the other and the seeds gradually spill down from one crate to another. This method, known as "the cascade," enables several tons of seeds to be fermented at a time.

When fermentation is over, the beans finally begin to have a recognizable cocoa smell. They must now be dried so that they acquire their final chocolate flavor. Ideally, the object is to reduce the bean's water content from 60 to 8 percent in order to prevent mildew. This operation must not take too long as the beans would rot, nor be too rapid, which would give them an acid flavor.

In most cacao-producing countries, the beans are dried naturally in the sun. They are spread out in colorful layers of brown, red, and caramel tones. On smaller plantations, they are spread out on mats laid directly on the bare ground, or on grids, wooden boards, or even cement paving stones. Workers are always on hand to cover them if the weather threatens to deteriorate. In South and Central America, the beans are spread on wooden flooring protected by sliding roofs, known in Trinidad as *boucan*, and as *baracas* in Brazil. When night falls, or if rain is announced,

they simply slide them across to protect the beans. For Jorge Amado, these drying places are "like ships ready to cross the ocean of golden trees." Sliding roofs are not employed in Africa. In certain regions, one comes across a particular type of drying apparatus known as the "omnibus," which consists of a series of drawers that can rapidly be slid under the shelter of roofs.

If it should rain or if the open-air drying methods prove inadequate, the beans are dried artificially. On large plantations, especially in Africa and Southeast Asia, electric dryers are used, or else they are dried over a fire. Care must be taken over the latter method, however, because if the beans come in contact with the fumes, they acquire a distinctive smoky taste and do not produce good chocolate.

The drying process usually takes one or two weeks. Throughout the entire operation, plantation workers, especially the women and children, turn the beans over in the sun, shifting them to ensure even drying. They sort them by hand, rake them over and remove the surplus pulp and debris. The women, dressed in their colorful madras fabrics, roll the beans between their fingers and discard the mildewed ones, which could contaminate the entire production. On some Caribbean islands, before the beans are completely dry they are moistened and then dried and turned once again. It was

On the small plantations of South and Central America and Africa, cacao seeds ferment slowly in enormous wicker baskets. Women endlessly tip them from one basket to another (above, São Tomé). On modern plantations, particularly in Indonesia, the baskets are replaced by large wooden fermentation crates with lattices. The seeds spill slowly down from one crate to another, gradually becoming flavorful cacao beans.

formerly said that this operation hardened them for the long journey ahead. Above all it gives them an incomparably smooth and brittle aspect. In Venezuela and Mexico, the beans used to be rolled in red earth or in ground brick, which gave them a bright, attractive color. In certain regions of South America, an ancient custom—the cacao dance—is still practised during the drying process. This is a dance without music, in which the dancers shuffle across the drying area, moving only their feet. "Dancing the cacao is an old tradition," explains chocolatier Christian Constant. "One encounters it in the Arriba region of Ecuador, where the celebrated '*nacional*' bean is turned during what is both the fermentation and drying phase, the only instance in which these two operations are carried out simultaneously, and a practice which is only suitable for a particular variety of cacao." Although this ancestral practice does not change the flavor of the beans, the dance removes surplus particles and improves the appearance of the beans by polishing them until they positively glisten. Some say it is a means of duping the buyers about their quality. Be that as it may, it is a fine tradition which Jorge Amado has described very poetically: "Under the sun, the cacao beans resemble glowing embers, on which the men dance, turning them over and over, so that the cacao will be superior cacao and not just 'good' or 'average'. . . They dance and sing, the beans burn their feet; at first they leave marks on the toes, then they get used to them. The hotter the sun, the better the cacao will be. It will look like burnished gold, like the men's faces, and it will smell of chocolate."

A field worker in Trinidad carries a basketful of seeds on his head (facing page). The fermented seeds are still very bitter. They gradually acquire their characteristic chocolate flavor after drying in the sun. Brazilian photographer Sebastião Salgado tried to capture the dignity of the plantation workers through his forceful images, whose impact is enhanced by the contrast between light and intense shadow. He immortalized these anonymous men who, in the stifling heat, unflaggingly turn the freshly harvested seeds over and over to ensure the optimum development of the cacao bean's aroma (above).

EN ROUTE FOR EUROPE

The beans have turned brown in the sun. Their aroma has become more marked and their fat content, that is to say the cocoa butter, is nearly 50 percent. The beans have been cleaned, relieved of all excess particles and are ready for the final process of sifting, during which they are graded. Jacques Brunel, a journalist who watched this operation in Trinidad, vividly described this moment of truth. "In a rickety shed with old registers piled up in the dust, an antiquated machine, half wood, half metal, sucks in the beans with a humming noise. Inside the machine there is a revolving cylinder where warm air propels them according to size towards seven compartments. The flat or puny beans, destined to end up ignominiously as cocoa butter or powder, are directed towards the first four compartments. The other three receive a shower of good plump beans." These are the beans which are reserved for the great chocolate makers. "Today, grading is carried out in many places by means of cylinders with perforations of various sizes," explains chocolate maker Christian Constant. "This selection of beans by size enables the somewhat inferior products to be rejected."

The beans are then transferred into hermetically sealed jute sacks and lined up in cool, airy warehouses, ready to be dispatched to ports or local markets. They need to be transported as soon as possible to avoid, in particular, the damage that vermin and insects can cause in these tropical climates. However, the quality of the beans still has to be checked and this can only be evaluated by cutting the beans open. This method of verification has now been adopted by the majority of the producer countries.

In Ghana this method has been used by the government since 1927. This country, a pioneer in the field, was the world's leading producer for many years. It is one of the few countries to have taken steps to maintain a fixed price for cacao beans in world markets. Due largely to its quality controls, Ghana produces some of the best African forasteros.

The first inspection takes place on the plantation just after the sacks have been filled. Government inspectors take samples from three hundred different sacks, using a pointed horn about 20 inches long. The beans are then placed in the hollows of a honeycomb board or table. They are opened lengthwise, either by hand, or by means of a special apparatus called a *magra*, which functions like a guillotine. The inspectors examine them, then classify them by grades according to their appearance.

Top quality, fully fermented beans are brown inside and, being the best, are the most expensive. These "fine grade" beans (criollos and trinitarios) are used to make the finest chocolate. The forasteros provide most of the "ordinary" cacao beans, which, depending on their region of production, can be further classified into second category beans, which are brownish purple inside, or third category, which are purple. Three further inspections are generally carried out, the first before the beans leave the plantation, the next on arrival in port, and the final one just before loading.

As a general rule beans are not transformed into chocolate in their country of

In the Caribbean islands, chocolate is still prepared in the traditional way: the mixture is made into sticks, like these being sold at a market in Trinidad (facing page). Everyone has a secret method of making them. One of the many recipes recommends drying the beans, roasting them in the oven, shelling them, reducing them to paste and then adding cinnamon, nutmeg, vanilla, a little milk, and some sugar. This mixture should then be boiled in water and the resulting paste kneaded. The chocolate is now ready to be eaten.

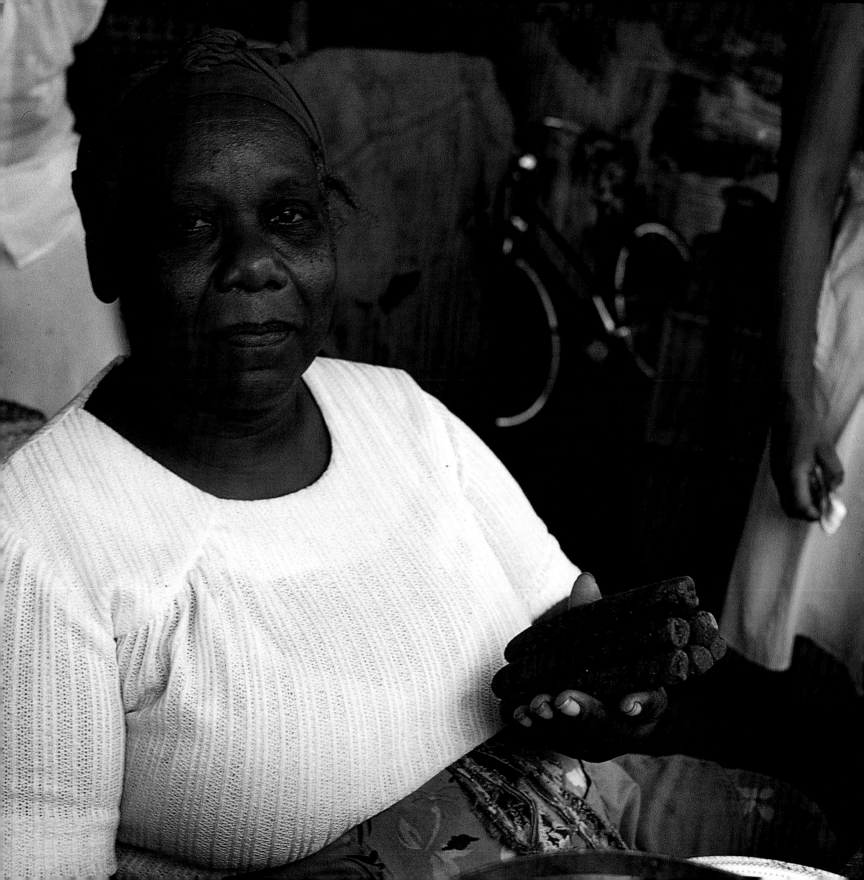

origin. Making chocolate involves a series of delicate operations and the skillful blending of the many varieties of beans. The prestige and quality of a chocolate also depends on the proportion of sugar and other additional ingredients, such as milk or vanilla. Each chocolate manufacturer has his own secret blending formulas.

Some countries, such as Brazil, the Ivory Coast, Cameroon, Malaysia, and Ecuador, now possess factories and have started to produce their own chocolate. Brazil produces cocoa paste, butter, and powder. However such initiatives are still the exception. Blending several varieties of beans which have come from different plantations often causes the cocoa paste to lack character. Although this is acceptable for industrial chocolate, it is quite unsuitable for the leading chocolate manufacturers. First-class beans are the basis of good chocolate. The ultimate quality of the chocolate depends on the quality of the beans and the skill with which they are blended.

Buyers always choose their batches with extreme care. Some chocolate manufacturers insist on selecting their beans on site. Their buyers are inveterate travelers who visit plantations in America, Africa, and Asia, where they inspect the growing conditions, harvesting, fermentation, and drying in order to choose the best produce. They also instruct small planters in the rules of hygiene and the latest methods of cultivating and preparing the beans. These chocolate "gringos," to use journalist Mariella Righini's term, scour plantations looking for the right crop. Valrhona,

Fermented, dried and graded cacao beans are put in sacks and stored in warehouses, like this one in the Ivory Coast (above), ready to leave the land of sun and tropical rain. In the middle of the sixteenth century, when these products were still unknown to many Europeans, it is said that the pirates who unwittingly seized these cargoes used to throw them overboard.

for example, the prestigious French chocolate manufacturer, employs a permanent representative in the tropics. He is in direct contact with planters and visits various plantations in order to choose the best ones in a given geographic zone. Valrhona adopts the philosophy and language of wine and vineyards, making grand crus chocolates which are linked to specific regions of production and which clearly express the concept of *terroir*.

However, planters do not usually sell their produce directly to chocolate manufacturers. Their beans are bought in the country of production, either by private import-export traders at non-regulated prices, or at regulation prices by government bodies which buy all or part of the country's production, which is the case in Venezuela, the Dominican Republic, and Trinidad. Cacao beans are subsequently sold to specialized negotiators, who act as suppliers to chocolate manufacturers. As with all raw materials, cacao beans are subject to supply and demand. Major stock exchanges set world rates in commodities markets. Listings in the markets in New York, Amsterdam, Paris and, above all, the London Stock Exchange serve as references. London is traditionally the reference for cacao beans from Africa and Southeast Asia, and New York the reference for American-grown cacao beans. The prices on these futures markets are subject to considerable fluctuations resulting from supply and demand forecasts.

The E.D. & F. Mann group, headquartered in London, is unique in the cacao world. It purchases cacao beans in West Africa and Southeast

These sacks awaiting exportation to European chocolate manufacturers are stored in cool, airy buildings ready for loading onto cargo vessels. The most aromatic beans come from the cacao tree's native lands (Ecuador, Central America, Colombia, and Venezuela). Those produced on the African continent or in Brazil are generally somewhat inferior, being robust and rather lacking in flavor; it is often said that they are to chocolate what the robusta coffee bean is to coffee.

Asia, and sells them to chocolate manufacturers all over the world. The company has representatives to supervise production and control harvest quality in the principal cacao-producing countries. Their opinions and comments at the local level are very important, since the quality of beans grown on the same plantation can vary, depending on the seasons and processing techniques. The studies made by the group's representatives enable E.D. & F. Mann to assess the quality of the beans in advance, anticipate world prices and speculate on the harvests. Furthermore, advice from representatives is greatly appreciated by planters, who are always ready to improve their production.

The cycle of the cacao beans in their native lands is at an end. In American, African, or Asian ports, jute sacks pile up on the docks. Historically, the first real cargo of cacao beans arrived in Spain in 1585. Europeans were soon to become infatuated with this astonishing product, until then totally unknown to them. The large galleons crossing the Atlantic to bring the riches of the New World to Europe were among the most sophisticated vessels of the day. Their vast holds could contain nearly 800 tons of merchandise and their rounded contours made them remarkably seaworthy. They were followed by the clippers, those fabulous vessels designed for crossing the seas in record time.

Today, freighters transport cacao beans to the great ports of Europe and North America. Sack after sack of this tropical harvest disappears into the ships' holds. The long voyage across the ocean is imminent, and all over the world chocolate makers impatiently await the arrival of the precious cargo.

Great chocolate manufacturers choose their beans in the same way as a wine-maker chooses his grape varieties. To them, the contents of these carefully selected sacks, coming from the far reaches of the earth (above, from the Ivory Coast), represent the world's most precious treasures. Giorgio Peyrano, the best and most celebrated chocolate maker in Turin, inspects a shipment of beans from Trinidad that has arrived in his factory (facing page).

· THE ·
HISTORY
· OF ·
CHOCOLATE

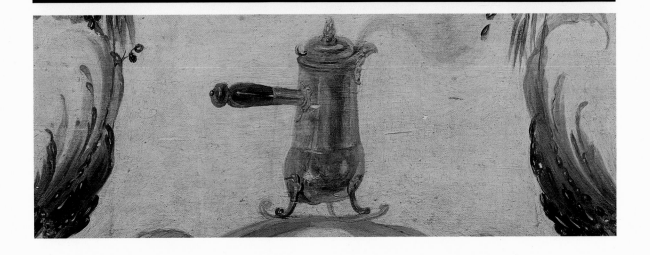

The origins of chocolate are shrouded in the mists of time. Its history begins in the heart of a continent which was not yet called South America, where the dense, equatorial virgin forest crossed by wide rivers was filled with the uninterrupted music of myriad insects, monkeys, and birds. Here, in the shady, humid environment under the forest's vast protective canopy of foliage grew smaller trees with pale slender trunks, dark green leaves, yellow flowers, and large fruits resembling gourds.

In the earliest times, these fruits were a treasure for small animals, who opened them up to eat the white pulp coating the seeds inside. By transporting the fruits and discarding the seeds, the animals of this forest, which stretched from the Orinoco to the Amazon river basin, gradually extended the domain of the cacao tree until it covered an area reaching from what is now Mexico in the north to what is now Guyana in the south. One day, the fruit was chanced upon by humans, who found its tangy pulp nutritious and delicious. From then on, the fruit became a regular element in the diet of the people of this region. Later, perhaps by chance, they discovered what could be obtained from the beans once they had been dried in the sun, roasted over the fire, and ground between two stones. No one, however, will ever know exactly where, when, and by what miracle chocolate really came into being.

QUETZALCOATL'S TREASURE

Between this discovery and the first organized cultivation of cacao trees, several centuries and perhaps even several millennia of prehistory elapsed. The Maya, who had settled in a region north of the equator in Central America, south of present-day Mexico, were the first civilization to leave behind durable, majestic vestiges. The first traces of the occupation of Maya territory date back to before 1000 B.C. Two thousand years later, or one thousand years before the discovery of this part of the New World by Europeans, Maya civilization was at its apogee. The magnificently built and sculpted stone palaces and temples today reveal few of their mysteries, but they are still almost intact, bearing witness to the splendor of this people. It was probably in the country of the Maya, stretching from the Yucatán peninsula to the Chiapas and the Pacific coast of Guatemala, that farmers started to cultivate the cacao tree for the first time. Legend has it that the cultivation of cacao was developed by Hunahpu, the third Maya king. According to some documents, it also appears that the Maya used cacao beans as a form of currency, and that cacao taxes were levied on the towns by the last princes of the empire. Perhaps this tax was one of the causes of its mysterious collapse and of the peasant uprisings during the tenth

This fifteen-hundred-year-old Maya vessel still contained some chocolate residue when it was discovered in 1984 in Guatemala. The image on the lid is the Maya symbol for chocolate (above). The cultivation of the cacao tree, precisely drawn, with its pods, in this pre-Columbian codex, was subsequently developed by the Aztecs (facing page). A few centuries later, silver chocolate pots and porcelain cups were to lend refinement to the pleasure of drinking chocolate. Page 58: a still life by François Desportes (1661–1743); page 59: detail from a mural by Christophe Huet dating from 1735.

century. The fall of the Maya empire remains one of the greatest enigmas of all history. Invaders from the north, the Toltecs, themselves driven from their capital by invading nomadic tribes, took over the territory of the fallen civilization, bringing with them their arts, technology, and gods. Among the latter figured Quetzalcoatl, who at the outset was a mere king. His destiny, or rather his legend, in which cacao had a role to play, was to change the course of history.

Long before he was elevated to the status of god in the Aztec pantheon, Topiltzin Quetzalcoatl was a peaceful man who was the political and religious leader of the Toltec tribe in the tenth century. He decided to set up his capital in Tula, or *Tollan* (literally, "place of reeds"), in northern Mexico. It is known that internal conflicts obliged Quetzalcoatl to flee the capital with his followers and emigrate south, finally settling in the Maya town of Chichén Itzá in Yucatán. Shortly after this, Quetzalcoatl was deified and the legend of his exile became a part of

Aztec mythology, which dominated the whole of pre-Columbian Mexico from the fourteenth century. This myth was related by Bernardino de Sahagún, a Spanish chronicler and author of a history of New Spain which was published in 1590. First he described the treasures that Quetzalcoatl possessed in Tollan. "All the riches of the world in gold and silver, in green stones known as chalchiuitl and in other precious materials, as well as an abundance of cacao trees of various colors. . . . The fortune of Quetzalcoatl and the Toltecs came to an end when three hostile necromancers appeared." One of them persuaded the ailing monarch to drink a mysterious beverage that would cure him, whereas in fact it drove him insane and incited him to leave his kingdom. He journeyed to the east coast where he found a raft made of intertwined snakes. He sailed away aboard this small craft.

But before leaving, Quetzalcoatl, now in the guise of the plumed serpent god, had promised to return during a year falling under

As a result of the Spanish conquest, chocolate would eventually spread to all the other continents. However, in conquering the Aztec empire, Hernán Cortés and his men were to strike a fatal blow against one of the most brilliant civilizations of all history, over which reigned gods of extraordinary appearance (right: the god Quetzalcoatl depicted in a codex). Sometimes, on the road to Tenochtitlán, the Aztec capital, the encounter between the two worlds took place peacefully (above: an illustration from a Spanish manuscript showing the arrival of Cortés in Tlaxcala).

the sign of *Ce-acatl*, "one reed." He would return to the same place from which he had left to recover his kingdom, bringing with him all the treasures of Paradise. In the Aztec calendar, 1519 was a *Ce-acatl* year. When the Aztec emperor, Montezuma II, heard of the arrival that year on the west coast of his territory of a vessel full of men whose armor shone in the sun like serpent's scales, crowned with plumed helmets, he imagined it to be the return of the god, and so he bade him welcome and gave him back his kingdom. In reality the god was Hernán Cortés who had come to plunder the West Indies and overthrow one of the most prestigious of all civilizations. By returning to earth and becoming part of history, the Quetzalcoatl myth changed the future of the New World.

Wicker baskets filled with cacao beans, the importance of which the Spanish soon understood, were among the gifts which the Aztecs offered to the conquistadors (above: an illustration from *Histoire de l'Amérique*, by De Bry, published in 1600 in Frankfurt). In addition, Cortés and his men also received provisions, magnificent garments made of cotton and feathers, gold jewelry, and even young slaves (one of these, Malinche, became the interpreter and later the faithful companion of Cortés, to whom she gave a son).

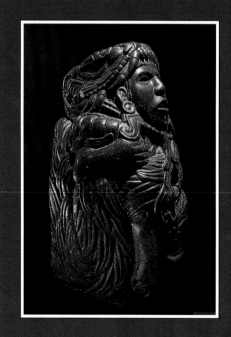

THE "TCHOCOLATL" OF THE NEW WORLD

Cortés and his men were not the first Europeans to discover the country of the Aztecs and cacao, one of its treasures. That exploit must of course be attributed to Christopher Columbus, who, during his fourth and last voyage to the region, reached the island of Guanaja—which he named Isla de Pinos—off the coast of Honduras, on 30 July 1502. The *Santa Maria* was nearing this unknown land when the crew noticed a large vessel put out to sea and head in their direction. Columbus had never seen such a large indigenous boat. There were no less than twenty-five oarsmen aboard, commanded by a chief wearing a magnificent embroidered coat and feathered headdress, seated in the center of the vessel under a canopy. As soon as it had drawn alongside the *Santa Maria*, the Aztecs climbed aboard, hoisting gifts of welcome onto the bridge, among which were fabrics, weapons made of wood, copper objects, and a large sack containing curious brown beans. After parleying for a while, Columbus gathered that the chief was ready to exchange these beans for some of the merchandise aboard. Seeing the foreigners' perplexity, the Aztecs gave them to understand that a delicious beverage could be prepared from these

beans. To illustrate their point, the chief had some prepared there and then by his servants. They ground some beans, mixed them with a variety of ingredients, and added some water. Columbus tasted it, but found the beverage very spicy and bitter. The Aztecs left with some glassware and the Genoese navigator continued along his route without taking the slightest interest in the sack of beans. He died four years later without knowing the destiny awaiting this bitter beverage, which the Aztecs called *tchocolatl*.

Seventeen years later, in 1519, Hernán Cortés, at the head of a flotilla of eleven vessels, landed on the coast of Tabasco, west of the Yucatán peninsula. He commanded an army of seven hundred men armed with harquebuses and fourteen cannons. On the Thursday before Easter, 21 April, Cortés and his men reached San Juan de Ulua, a site discovered the previous year by the Spanish navigator, Juan de Grijalva. They had scarcely anchored when two large pirogues drew up alongside bringing envoys from the Aztec emperor, Montezuma, who had come to sound out the intentions of the Spaniards. Over the next days, other important, magnificently attired and bejeweled imperial dignitaries came to make contact with Cortés. Realizing the riches which this Aztec land harbored, Cortés decided to march on their capital,

It was a continent rich in chocolate that Europeans were to discover and geographers to chart (facing page, top: a map of the Atlantic Ocean drawn by Pierre de Vaulx in 1613). During his conquest, Cortés was helped by the coincidence between the myth of the god Quetzalcoatl and his own arrival in Tenochtitlán, which led the Aztecs to regard him as the reincarnation of their god (facing page, bottom: pre-Columbian statuette of the god). As for the emperor Montezuma, his passion for chocolate, which he shared with all the Aztec dignitaries, inspired awe-struck descriptions on the part of contemporary chroniclers (above: an anonymous eighteenth-century portrait).

Tenochtitlán. He had all of his vessels burned to prevent desertions and set off. After a few months punctuated by combats with tribes terrorized by the cannons, Cortés reached the gates of the city. The Spaniards marveled at the magnificence they found inside. Montezuma greeted Cortés in these terms: "Because of the faith we have in our beliefs, we are certain that you are the men our ancestors spoke of, who were to come from where the sun rises. You will have at your disposal everything you need, because here you are at home in your native country." The emperor immediately offered Cortés the revenue from a vast plantation of cacao trees. The beans of this plant served as currency in Montezuma's empire, and so, unlike Columbus, Cortés quickly came to understand the economic value of cacao.

In their accounts, the earliest travelers stressed the importance the Aztecs attached to cacao and to chocolate, the beverage they made from it. "Cacao" and "chocolate" are two words whose etymology seems irrefutable; the first derives from the Aztec word *cacahuatl*, denoting the substance which was extracted from the beans of the *cacahuacintli*, itself the fruit of the *cacahuaquahuitl*, the cacao tree. As for the second word, it is the universal transcription of the Maya word *tchocolatl*, or more precisely, *xocolatl*. Thomas Gage, an English Dominican friar who lived in the West Indies from 1625 to 1637, devoted a considerable part of his work, *A New Survey of the West-India's*, to chocolate, for which he proposed a picturesque etymology: "This name Chocolate is a *Indian* name, and is compounded from Atte, as some say or as others, Alte, which in the *Mexican* language signifieth water & from the sound which the water (wherein is put the Chocolate) makes, as Choco, Choco, Choco, when it is stirred in a cup by an instrument called a Molinet, or Molinillo, until it bubble and rise into a froath."

In November 1519, after destroying his fleet to prevent desertions (above: the scene as depicted by the Spanish painter, Rafael Monleón, in 1887) and achieving a few military victories, Cortés was received by Montezuma as if he were Quetzalcoatl himself returning after a long exile: "Welcome to you, our master, on your return to your country among your own people, to sit on your throne. . . ." The numerous gifts which the emperor offered Cortés included a cacao tree plantation. Facing page: drawing by Miguel González (1698) depicting Cortés's arrival at the court of Montezuma.

The Aztecs controlled a vast area devoted to cacao cultivation, which stretched across southern Mexico as far as Guatemala. However, production was not sufficient, nor the plantations close enough to towns, for chocolate to be a common beverage throughout the empire. It was indeed the product's relative rarity which raised it to the rank of currency, much the same as gold and silver in the Old World. Cacao beans were used for various transactions. A pumpkin cost four beans, a rabbit was worth ten, twelve were required for the services of a prostitute, and one hundred for the purchase of a slave. Larger units existed to facilitate the payment of important sums. For example, twenty-four thousand beans constituted a *carga*, the maximum load a man could carry on his back (about 65 pounds). It was of course in *cargas* that towns and provinces had to pay their annual tribute to Tenochtitlán, a total estimated at around a hundred tons of beans. Since cacao beans are perishable, it is probable that the Aztec state rapidly converted the beans into various types of merchandise, retaining a certain amount to be consumed by princes, high ranking officials, and priests, as well as offerings to the gods.

Apart from those living in cacao-producing regions, ordinary people never drank chocolate. The rare beverage was reserved for important people and, during certain festivities, for merchants. According to historian Bernal Díaz del Castillo, a companion of Cortés, the emperor drank it every day. In his *The Discovery and Conquest of Mexico*, he described the emperor's dinner in the following terms: "He sat on a low, richly decorated, comfortable seat. The table also was low and crafted in the same style as the chairs. It was covered with white tablecloths and a few small, narrow napkins made of the same fabric. Four very beautiful and impeccably clothed women brought him hand basins. . . . At the same time hand towels were offered to him, and two other women

Chocolate was a luxury for the Aztecs and cacao beans, like gold, were a rare commodity which served both as currency and as gifts for kings and gods. The magnificent frieze *The History of Mexico* in the Palacio Nacional in Mexico City, painted by the Mexican painter Diego Rivera, includes this section showing offerings of fruit, tobacco, cacao beans, and vanilla being presented to the emperor (facing page). One of the illustrations from *Histoire de l'Amérique*, by De Bry (1600), portrayed Aztecs loading and carrying a tribute consisting, in part, of cacao pods (above).

immediately brought him cornbread pancakes. When he commenced his meal, a sort of gilded screen was placed in front of him, so that he was not visible while eating. . . . From time to time, fine gold cups were brought to him containing a beverage made from cacao. It was said to have aphrodisiac properties, but we did not pay any attention to this detail. What I did see was about fifty large mugs of a very frothy beverage made of cacao being served. . . . After the monarch, it was the turn of the soldiers of his guard and other persons in his retinue to dine. Something like a thousand servings in all . . . More than two thousand mugs of frothy cacao in the traditional way the Mexicans prepare it were served."

The Aztecs regarded the cacao tree as a sacred plant, and religious ceremonies were held to mark the various phases of its cultivation. Apart from the dances and offerings in honor of the goddesses of food and water, special rites were performed at the time of sowing, which involved exposing the best seeds to moonlight for four nights before they were planted. The night preceding the sowing, the planters, who for thirteen days had been observing ritual celibacy, returned to their wives to give free rein to their desires.

CACAO, CHILI, AND SPICES

Many travelers have left detailed descriptions of the way in which the Aztecs cultivated cacao and prepared chocolate. The first of these, Girolamo Benzoni, published a work in Venice in 1565, *Historia del Mondo Nuovo*, which is one of the liveliest descriptions of that era. Benzoni was a botanist who visited the Americas from 1541 to 1555, at the very beginning of their colonization.

The first colonists found the generally unsweetened chocolate drunk by the Aztecs repugnant. Nevertheless numerous travelers gave detailed accounts of the manner in which the Aztecs prepared it. First the dried beans were ground, then the flour was transformed into paste, which was diluted in hot water with chilies, and then the beverage was shaken, skimmed and beaten with a molinet until it was frothy. This sixteenth-century anonymous engraving shows inhabitants of New Spain on a plantation carrying out the various steps involved in turning cacao beans into drinking chocolate.

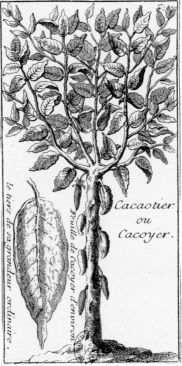

Cacaotier ou Cacoyer.

"They call the fruit *cacauate* and use it for money. The tree on which it grows is not very tall, and only thrives in hot, shady places, as even minimal exposure to the sun kills it. For this reason they normally plant them in the damp areas of forests. Fearing that this might not suffice, they plant another taller tree next to it to protect it from the sun. . . . The almond-shaped *cacauate* fruit is concealed in a sort of gourd almost as large as a cucumber. They take a year to ripen. And when they are in season, they pick them, and, having drained them, spread them out on mats or bamboo grids to dry in the sun.

"The Indians make a beverage from it and this is how they proceed: they take as many fruits as they need and put them in an earthenware pot and dry them over the fire. Then they break them between two stones and reduce them to flour just as they do when they make bread. They then transfer this flour into vessels made of gourd halves (the gourds that they drink from are to be found on trees growing throughout the Indies), moisten the flour gradually with water, often adding their 'long pepper,' and then they drink it."

This was the simple method commonly employed by the Aztecs for preparing chocolate, at the time when their empire had just been destroyed forever by the conquistadors. It is interesting to note that Benzoni describes the vessels used by the Aztecs as simple, scooped out shells of fruits such as the coconut. Only a few years later, however, Bernardino de Sahagún spoke of "beautiful vases decorated with various paintings depending on their place of origin, with tortoise-shell lids and matching spoons to whisk the cocoa." The Aztecs did in fact often beat the liquid before drinking it, not so much to make it frothy, but to bring the fat to the surface so that they could skim it off. But whatever the container, the most common chocolate at that time was simply a mixture of cocoa and "long pepper," in other words chili. It is hardly surprising that it did not immediately appeal to the Spaniards. Further on Benzoni reveals, through an account of his own experiences, how chocolate finally came to be accepted by the colonists. "Sometimes, when passing through a village, I would come across an Indian who would offer me a drink of chocolate. I would refuse it, the Indian would be most astonished by my refusal, then laugh, and go on his way. In the long run, finding myself often in places where there was not a drop of wine, I learned to do as the others, so that I would not be drinking only water all the time. Its taste is not all bitter, it

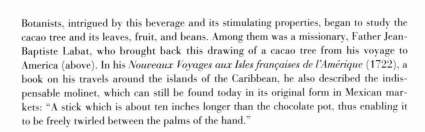

Botanists, intrigued by this beverage and its stimulating properties, began to study the cacao tree and its leaves, fruit, and beans. Among them was a missionary, Father Jean-Baptiste Labat, who brought back this drawing of a cacao tree from his voyage to America (above). In his *Nouveaux Voyages aux Isles françaises de l'Amérique* (1722), a book on his travels around the islands of the Caribbean, he also described the indispensable molinet, which can still be found today in its original form in Mexican markets: "A stick which is about ten inches longer than the chocolate pot, thus enabling it to be freely twirled between the palms of the hand."

nourishes and refreshes the body, and is not intoxicating."

If Benzoni, the zealous convert, was quick to assert that the Aztec's chocolate was not bitter, that is because it was, of course. Without any sugar, and merely a dose of chili, it could hardly have been otherwise. However, his description of this simple preparation only concerns the rustic method of preparing chocolate employed by the peasants he met when "passing through a village" in cacao-producing regions. In Thomas Gage's description of the way in which the Aztecs prepared chocolate, he indicated the presence of other ingredients: "But the meaner set of people, as *Blackamoors* and *Indians*, commonly put nothing in it, but *Cacao*, *Achiotte*, *Maize*, and a few *Chilies* with a little Aniseed." To this list of ingredients, Sahagun added an important element: "Sometimes they add aromatic spices and even bees' honey." This was probably for the chocolate reserved for merchants, dignitaries, and princes, a spicy beverage with the subtle flavors of vanilla and aniseed, sometimes thickened with a corn hash and sweetened with honey.

Whatever the method of preparation, the Indians appreciated chocolate for its nutritious and stimulating properties. Already in Cortés's day, Díaz del Castillo referred to its aphrodisiac properties, which played a considerable role in the success it encountered in Europe in the seventeenth century. We do not know to what extent the Aztecs believed in these properties, but it is certain that they knew how to use chocolate as a stimulant both for the mind and the spirit, and they sometimes mixed it with other medicinal plants. Furthermore, they had discovered another use for cacao: for certain religious rites they made a paste with it which they painted on their faces. This can be seen as an early use of plants for cosmetic ends, a practice which, along with chocolate preparation in general, was subsequently to be considerably modified by the New World colonists.

VOYAGE
DE THOMAS GAGE.
Tome. II.   *Aveline fecit*

In Europe, the discovery of chocolate and other indigenous customs owed much to Thomas Gage, an English Dominican friar who lived in the West Indies for twenty-four years. After his first visit, from 1625 to 1637, he published a work entitled *A New Survey of the West-India's* (above: the frontispiece illustration of the second volume of a French edition).

SWEETENED CHOCOLATE: A COLONIAL PASSION

Father Labat, who gave a detailed account of his 1720 mission to the West Indies, or the "French islands of America," as he called the region in his work *Nouveaux Voyages aux isles françaises de l'Amérique*, reported that the Creole population in Martinique frequently employed the expression *à la chicolade*, meaning eight o'clock in the morning. The expression referred to a firmly rooted custom that had taken hold a century earlier. Chocolate had become a daily beverage for the new Americans, irrespective of their social status. However, in order to find favor with the colonists, chocolate had had to undergo a considerable change. This consisted of adding sugar to the mixture, without which chocolate would probably have disappeared. As soon as they had settled in America, the Spanish planted sugar cane from the Canary Islands in Mexico and in Hispaniola, the island of present-day Haiti and the Dominican Republic. The first European settlers in Mexico decided to add sugar to cocoa to soften its bitterness, thereby making chocolate a far more enjoyable beverage. From that point on, their infatuation with sweetened chocolate spread rapidly to other conquered territories and was a factor in the development of sugar plantations.

In Mexico in the 1630s, the Dominican friar Thomas Gage witnessed the Spaniards' passion for sweet chocolate, which they sometimes drank in specialized public establishments which were known as *chocolaterias*. The recipe contained quite a few of the original *tchocolatl* ingredients, but was decidedly more sophisticated. "As for the rest of the ingredients which

Chocolate, unlike tobacco, which was discovered by the Europeans at the same period, was immediately perceived as beneficial. This allegorical illustration adorning a work on chocolate published in Latin in 1639 portrays an Aztec requesting Neptune to make the beneficial effects of chocolate known to the world (above).

make this Chocolattical confection, there is a notable variety; for some put into it black Pepper, which is not well approved by the Physitians. . . . It is further compounded with white Sugar, Cinnamon, Clove, Anniseed, Almonde, *Hazellnuts, Orejuela, Baiulla, Sapoyoll,* Orenge flower water, some Muske, and as much of achiotte, as will make it looke of the colour of red bricke." Further on, Thomas Gage indicated the quantities they generally used, one hundred beans necessitating the addition of half a pound of sugar. Cacao was processed according to the Aztec method which called for drying, then grinding on a stone known as a *metate*. However, the next phase of preparation seems to point to an improvement on the technique described by Benzoni seventy years earlier.

Cacao and various ingredients ground into powder were slowly heated in a recipient over a fire until they formed a creamy paste. Thomas Gage explained that "When it is well beaten, and incorporated (which will be known by the shortnesse of it) then with a spoon (so in the *India's* is used) is taken up some of the paste, which will be almost liquid, and made into tablets, or else without a spoon put into boxes, and when it is cold it will be hard. Those that make it into tablets, put a spoonefull of the paste upon a peece of paper (the *Indians* put it on a leaf of a plantintree) where, being put into the shade (for in the sunne it melts and dissolves) it growes hard; and then bowing the paper or the leaf, the tablet falls off, by reason of the fatnesse of the paste. . . . But the most ordinary way, is, to

This still life painting by Francisco de Zurbarán (1598–1664) suggests that for its first European aficionados chocolate was more a healthy, nutritious food, than a simple pleasure. However, for the church it remained a beverage, not a food, and provided an ideal means of enduring religious fasts. Moreover, chocolate was often made in convents and monasteries, according to ancient Mesoamerican methods which remained in use until the eighteenth century (opposite: the grinding of beans, Mesoamerican fashion, on a concave stone slab).

warme the water very hot, and then to powre out halfe the cup full that you mean to drinke; and to put into it a tablet of two, or as much as will thicken reasonably the water, and then grind it well with the Molinet, and when it is ground and risen to a scum, to fill the cup with hot water, and so drinke it by sups (having sweetened it with Sugar) and to eat it with a little conserve, or maple bread, steeped into the Chocolate." This preparation contained innovations other than the mere addition of sugar. At that time, chocolate tablets, no doubt perfected by the Spaniards, were not yet intended for eating, but solid chocolate facilitated storage, transportation, and preparation with hot water. The New World Spaniards invented hot chocolate, which was unknown to the Aztecs, and bread sticks for dipping. The Spanish "make toasted bread fingers," wrote Father Labat, "or special biscuits, which they dip in their chocolate."

Thomas Gage was amazed by the vogue for chocolate which prevailed in Mexico among the Spaniards at the beginning of the seventeenth century. The Dominican father was staying in the Mexican town of Chiapa when he witnessed a tragic incident caused by this passion for chocolate. His account offers us a spicy insight into the morals of the day. "The woman of that City it seems pretend much weaknesse and squeamishnesse of stomack, which they say is so great, that they are not able to continue in the Church while a Mass is briefly hudled over, much less while a solemn high Masse (as they call it) is sung, and a Sermon preached, unless they drink a cup of hot Chocolate, and eat a bit of sweet-meats to strengthen their stomackes. For this purpose it was much used by them to make their maids bring to them a cup of hot Chocolate . . . The Bishop perceiving this abuse, and having given faire warning for the omitting of it, but all without amendment, thought it fit to fixe in writing upon the Church dores an excommunication against all such as should presume at the time of service to eat or drinke within the Church." Thereupon the women decided, on the contrary, to openly scorn the excommunication edict and to drink even more chocolate in church. One day in Chiapa, the men drew their swords against the priests and canons who attempted to snatch the chocolate away from the ladies. Seeing that the situation was hopeless and that their ministry was becoming impossible, the clergy decided to abandon the town church. From then on services took place in those churches and convents where the monks permitted the ladies to drink as they pleased. At this juncture the bishop fell seriously ill and eventually died. "A gentlewoman with whom I was well acquainted in that City, who was noted to be somewhat too familiar with one of the Bishops Pages, was commonly censured to have prescribed such a cup of Chocolate to be minstered by the Page which poysoned him . . . And it afterwards became a Proverbe in that Country, Beware of the Chocolate of *Chiapa* . . . The Women of this City . . . have

Having forbidden the consumption of chocolate during Mass, the unfortunate bishop of Chiapa in Mexico was murdered by one of the women churchgoers who, to exact revenge, put poison in his cup of chocolate! Thomas Gage witnessed this event in around 1630, and he related it in his treatise, *A New Survey of the West-India's*. An illustration which appears in one edition of the book (above) portrays Dom Bernard de Salazar visiting the Chiapa area: "The Spaniards and the Indians brought him their offerings while he confirmed their children."

LE BON USAGE

DU THÉ

DU CAFFÉ

ET

DU CHOCOLAT

POUR LA PRESERVATION

& pour la guerison des Maladies.

Par Mr DE BLEGNY, Conseiller, Medecin,
Artiste ordinaire du Roy & de Monsieur,
& préposé par ordre de sa Majesté, à la
Recherche & Verification des nouvelles
découvertes de Medecine.

A PARIS,

Chez
L'AUTEUR, au College des quatre Nations,
La Veuve D'HOURY, Quay des Augustins,
Et la Veuve NION, ruë des Mathurins.

M. DC. LXXXVII.

Avec Privilege du Roy.

learned from the Devil many enticing lessons and baits ... and if they cannot have their willes, they will surely work revenge either by Chocolate or Conserves, or some present, which shall surely carry death along with it."

This anecdote about Chiapa provides an illuminating insight into the Spaniards' infatuation with chocolate and the clergy's attitude towards the beverage. Unlike tobacco, another recently discovered indigenous delight, chocolate was never regarded by the church as a diabolical product. The bishop of Chiapa used to drink it, a habit which caused his downfall, and forbade it only during services. Not so the monks in monasteries, who, according to Thomas Gage, even tolerated it during Mass. Monks and nuns, in fact, were among the most fervent chocolate lovers, since the beverage made the fasts to which they were subjected far more bearable. Furthermore, they soon became specialists in the preparation of chocolate tablets that were subsequently sold to soldiers and colonists. The nuns of Oaxaca, for example, were renowned for their wonderful recipes for cinnamon and aniseed chocolate.

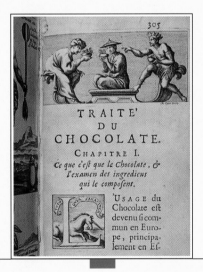

New World Spaniards, far from restricting themselves to the sweetest of drinking chocolates, also developed certain other properties of cacao. Thomas Gage described how a kind of butter was produced which the creole women rubbed on their faces to improve their complexions. Evidently the cosmetic value of cocoa butter was already appreciated in the seventeenth century, as it is today.

Well before chocolate consumption became widespread in the Old World, the Spaniards' infatuation for it, soon to be shared by all colonists throughout South America and the West Indies, was the driving force behind the development of cacao tree plantations. Cacao was relatively profitable as it was cheap to cultivate; the crops moreover fetched a good price, attracting numerous planters. The development of their activity, along with that of the sugar planters, was the cause of the plight of hundreds of thousands of Africans who were reduced to slavery. In 1720, Father Labat referred to this sinister aspect of the cacao economy before the abolition of slavery in chillingly pragmatic terms: "Several experiments have convinced me that twenty

This work by one of Louis XIV's doctors was published at a time when chocolate was all the rage at the French court (facing page). In England, the diarist Samuel Pepys, who drank his first cup of chocolate in 1662, found it an excellent remedy for the migraines and stomach aches brought on by the excessive consumption of wine at mealtimes. Philippe Sylvestre Dufour, in his *Traités nouveaux et curieux du café, du thé et du chocolat*, published in 1685 (above), spoke of the Mesoamerican custom of drinking vanilla-flavored chocolate (top).

Negroes can tend and cultivate fifty thousand cacao trees. . . . These fifty thousand well-tended trees will yield a hundred thousand pounds of almonds which, selling at seven sols and six deniers per pound . . . will earn thirty-seven thousand francs, a sum which is all the more appreciable because of the fact that almost all of it goes directly into the owner's pocket, due to the low cost of keeping the slaves who tend the trees. They constitute the one and only obligatory expense. . . . A cacao plantation is a veritable gold mine."

As early as 1568, a traveler spoke of two Spanish plantations in Mexico, one in Quesala and the other in Tecoanapa. Less than a century later, after developing rapidly on the mainland, the first plantations appeared on the islands of Hispaniola and Jamaica. In 1660, the French continued the trend by planting cacao trees in Martinique. Through close commercial ties with Mexico, the Philippines received their first cacao saplings in 1663. Plantations in Ecuador, Brazil, and Trinidad were not set up until the middle of the eighteenth century, followed by Africa in 1822. The growth in the number of cacao plantations was due, naturally, to the considerable success chocolate encountered in Europe.

The discovery of distant lands and hitherto unknown flavors meant that the sixteenth and seventeenth centuries were rich in new sensations. The great shipping companies transported exciting new products from the New World to revive the spirits of the inhabitants of the Old World (above: an illustration from a treatise on the East Indies by R. de Hoogn). Meanwhile, in the West Indies a new form of society emerged, with its masters and slaves, its languages, and its particular customs in which chocolate played an essential role (facing page: 1775 painting by Le Masurier depicting slaves taking refreshments in front of their hut).

IN THE LUGGAGE
OF SPANISH PRINCESSES

It is not known whether it was a traveler, a monk, or a soldier who brought the first cacao beans to Europe, but it was no doubt a Spaniard returning home shortly after the conquest. Cortés himself, who was called back to his native country in 1527, is said to have brought some back amongst his spoils, along with the appropriate utensils, as a gift for Charles V; however, there is no indication that the latter appreciated the beverage. From that time on, various Spaniards returning home from America introduced chocolate into their own circles, and probably continued to prepare it the way the Aztecs did. However, real development began in 1585 with the unloading of the first commercial cargo of cacao from Veracruz. From then on, regular transport was organized between the Spanish colonies in America and Spain. Chocolate was prepared in convents and monasteries, notably by the Jesuits, often with added spices, and soon reached the court and aristocratic households. In the seventeenth century, Madrid, the influential capital of Philip II's kingdom, became the center from which chocolate was to captivate Europe. It was already known in Flanders and the Netherlands (which had become Spanish territories a century earlier), and reached Italy in 1606, imported by a Florentine merchant, Antonio Carletti, who had discovered it while on business in Spain. The beverage became a resounding success on the Italian peninsula, and in the seventeenth century a number of *cioccolatieri* in Venice, Florence, and especially Perugia and Turin, became great specialists in the art of preparing cocoa. Italian chocolate masters began exporting their products to other European countries.

Nine years after its arrival in Italy, chocolate entered France in the luggage of a very young Spanish princess who had a passion for chocolate, the Infanta Anne of Austria, daughter of Philip III. At the age of fourteen, when

This mural dating from 1710 in the Museum of Ceramics in Barcelona captures the elegance and refinement of the Spanish aristocracy. A reception is being given in a magnificent garden laid out around a beautiful fountain. Some of the guests are dancing to the sound of musical instruments. The gentlemen are preparing hot drinks using sticks of chocolate and are serving them to the ladies. The chocolate pot in *Still-Life: Chocolate Service*, by Spanish artist Luis Menendez (1776), is made of copper and contains a molinet. Tablets of chocolate like those depicted in the bottom right-hand corner were dissolved in hot water to make the drink.

she married Louis XIII, a young king of the same age, she brought an army of servants, all of whom were chocolate enthusiasts and extremely skilled at preparing it, to the French court. The fashion for this beverage was thus launched, and it was all the more warmly accepted because it seemed to be an unusual eccentricity and a luxury reserved for a certain elite. Alphonse de Richelieu, cardinal of Lyon and brother of the celebrated minister, was among the first privileged few to experience this delight, and was to become an inveterate drinker of the beverage, which tempered the "vapors" of his spleen, calmed his anger, and dissipated his ill humor. Some time later, another cardinal, Mazarin, influenced perhaps by the queen, Anne of Austria, became so infatuated with chocolate that he recruited a personal chocolate maker from his native Italy. In 1660, the marriage of another Spanish princess, Maria Theresa of Austria, to Louis XIV marked a new phase in the enthusiasm

All the pleasures of chocolate are captured in this still life, dating from 1652, by Antonio de Pereda y Salgado, one of the most beautiful to be seen in the Hermitage Museum of St. Petersburg: the pleasure of novelty first of all, then that of preparing it with the appropriate instruments (one can distinguish the molinet, the chocolate pot with its lid with a hole in it, and the spoon for skimming and removing the cocoa butter), the pleasure of sweetened chocolate (a Spanish invention), and finally that of fried or toasted bread (picatoste) dipped in the delicious beverage. Today, chocolate is served in Spain with churros, long, sweet doughnuts which have replaced the picatoste.

for chocolate in France. The queen's love of chocolate was such that it was written of her that the king and chocolate were her only two passions. The chances are that the latter, being more faithful than the former, disappointed her less. Until then, chocolate had been reserved for the court, but, boosted by the queen's infatuation, it rapidly spread to all the best drawing rooms, which enabled France's first chocolate maker, David Chaillou, to make his fortune in Paris, after obtaining by patent letter from the king in 1659, "the exclusive privilege of making, selling and serving a certain composition known as chocolate."

David Chaillou had followed the example of an anonymous Frenchman who, in 1657, had opened the first English chocolate-house. That year, a London newspaper, the *Public Advertiser*, informed its readers that "In Bishopsgate Street, a French establishment offers an excellent West India drink called chocolate to be sold, where you may have it ready at any time and also unmade at reasonable rates." Whereas Chaillou simply followed a fashion which had originated in aristocratic salons, this unnamed pioneer launched it by making a previously unknown beverage available to the man in the street. So from the outset, chocolate in England was consumed much more democratically. A large number of chocolate-houses appeared in London, openly vying with coffee-houses. These two kinds of establishment were similar in that both were places where upper-class London society could eat and play cards in comfort, and above all have interminable discussions on the burning topics of the day. The most fashionable chocolate-house was indubitably White's, in St. James's Street, where one could also buy theater and opera tickets. It was rivaled by the Cocoa Tree, where politicians, particularly Tories, were in the habit of meeting.

During the first hundred years following its introduction into Europe, chocolate was

White's, which opened in 1697 in elegant St. James's Street, was one of London's most reputed chocolate-houses, where politics and love were discussed, wagers placed, and beer, coffee, and, above all, chocolate, were drunk (above: White's in 1708). The chocolate might well have been served in a *trembleuse* cup, invented at the beginning of the eighteenth century to prevent accidents: the cup was placed in the hollow of a special saucer, or, better still, was fitted with a holder (left: Spanish *trembleuse* cup dating from 1750).

mainly consumed as a stimulant, and the fact that it was not considered purely as a culinary pleasure sparked a number of controversies, the first of which was of a religious nature. As in the New World, chocolate was adopted in the first half of the sixteenth century by the monks and nuns of Spanish monasteries and convents, who saw in it an excellent way of enduring fasts, and gradually they became expert chocolate makers. However, some churchmen grew concerned: if chocolate was sufficiently nourishing to provide lengthy relief from hunger pangs, then it should be considered as food rather than drink, and therefore be forbidden during fasts. This delicate question was put to Pope Pius V in 1569. The great inquisitor, more indulgent than usual, replied, citing Saint Thomas, that chocolate was to all intents and purposes a beverage. In fact, for another one hundred years, the beverage acquired both new enthu-

siasts and new flavors, and the question continued to intrigue theologians and scholars. It was only in 1662 that Cardinal Francesco Maria Brancaccio pronounced the final verdict in the name of the church: "Beverages do not break fasts. Wine, nutritious as it is, does not break them. The same applies to chocolate. That it is nourishing we cannot deny, but by no means does it follow that it is a food."

The second debate was of a scientific order. As early as the sixteenth century, chocolate, a new and little-known substance whose effects on health were not obvious, was the subject of numerous medical theories and contradictory opinions and recommendations. During these pre-scientific centuries, when medicine was still in its infancy, there were endless debates concerning the "hot" or "cold" nature of the product. It was because the Spaniards considered it as "cold," that for a long time they persisted in adding pepper and various spices in

Trembleuse cup and gallant company: two typical images of the increasingly refined world of chocolate in the eighteenth century (above: a Spanish drawing, *La hora del chocolate*). Chocolate, the feminine drink *par excellence*, was also a stimulant, if not an aphrodisiac, suggesting delicious ambiguities. Facing page: In this portrait attributed to Charles Joseph Natoire (1700–1777), Mademoiselle de Charolais is disguised in a monk's attire. She has made a knot in Saint Francis's waist cord, and it is no coincidence that her cup of chocolate is nearby.

order to neutralize its supposedly morbid effects. While Father Labat congratulated them on this point ("it is because cocoa is cold that the Spaniards are right to add hot ingredients"), other voices in France firmly condemned them. "It is not surprising that Spanish women are thin," peremptorily declared Madame d'Aulnoy, a traveler at the end of the seventeenth century, "for nothing burns more than the chocolate they drink to excess. Furthermore, they season it inordinately with pepper and other spices as much as they are able, so that they are literally consumed by it. . . ."

However, this debate concerning the nature of the beverage did not prevent chocolate from growing in popularity. The majority of botanists and doctors contributed to this trend by analyzing the product and discovering all manner of beneficial properties. In 1591, Juan de Cardenas, one of the first Spanish doctors to study chocolate, vaunted its merits in a work about the peculiarities and marvels of the Indies, stating that the high fat content of chocolate had a positive effect on "animal heat." Thomas Gage emphasized its digestive virtues: "True it is, it is used in the *India's*, then in the *European* parts, because there the stomackes are more apt to faint then here, and a cup of Chocolate well confectioned comforts and strengthens the stomack." He went on to describe its stimulating properties: ". . . and when I was purposed to sit up late to study, I would take another cup about seven or eight at night which would keep me waking until about midnight." In 1684, a medical student named F. Foucault defended his dissertation on chocolate, entitled *Ad chocolatae usus salubris*. Doctor Bachot, chairman of the examining board, waxed eloquent on the subject of the beverage:"It is, more than nectar or ambrosia, the true food of the gods. . . ." As early as the seventeenth century, chocolate had won over nearly

Men preferred coffee and women preferred chocolate, but this difference formed no obstacle to courtly meetings, rendered all the more delectable by the aphrodisiac reputation of the beverage. Above: *Coffee and Chocolate*, an engraving by Johann Elias Rindinger (1698–1767). The delicious early morning hot chocolate which ladies drank in bed inspired a number of erotic bedroom scenes, such as this engraving by Noël le Mire (1724–1800) depicting a voluptuous gourmand, perhaps startled by the sound of footsteps (facing page, top). In Venice, ladies could buy their chocolate at La Nave, one of the confectioners in the San Marco district, whose letterhead can be seen here (facing page, bottom, *circa* 1700).

every heart. Nutritious, digestible, stimulating, even aphrodisiac, effective in curing hypochondria and consumption, good for the breath and the voice, such were the principal qualities attributed to this beverage made from the seeds of the plant called *Theobroma*, "food of the gods," the name devised in 1734 by the naturalist Linnaeus for cacao. In 1712, a certain Doctor Bligny went so far as to prescribe it for the common cold, pneumonia, diarrhea, dysentery, and even cholera!

Chocolate certainly also had its detractors, such as the Princess Palatine, who considered it to be poison, and Madame de Sévigné, who started by liking it, but later changed her mind. On 11 February 1671, the anxious marchioness wrote to her daughter, Madame de Grignan, who had just left Paris for Provence, in the south of France: "You say you are not feeling at all well and you have not slept a wink? Chocolate will put you right. But you do not own a chocolate pot; this has crossed my mind a thousand times. How will you manage?" By 13 May she had changed her mind. "I beg of you my very dear, good, loved one, not to drink any chocolate. I personally have taken a real dislike to it. Last week, I suffered for sixteen hours with colic and constipation which caused me as much pain as nephritis." However, Madame de Grignan, who was pregnant, took no notice of her mother's recommendations. On the contrary, she drank large quanti-

ties of chocolate and was very satisfied with it. This miraculous cure somewhat shook the marquise's conviction. "But on the subject of chocolate," she wrote on 25 October, "are you not afraid of heating the blood? All these miraculous effects, do you not think that they conceal something that might flare up?" The following day, emboldened by her daughter's encouraging remarks, she gave way to temptation and then related the event on 28 October. "I wanted to be reconciled with chocolate; I took some night before last to digest my dinner in order to have a good supper. I took some yesterday for sustenance so that I might fast until evening. It had all the effects on me I wanted; that is why I find chocolate agreeable, because it acts according to one's wishes." The reconciliation was, alas, short-lived. In January, after her daughter had given birth to a slightly feverish baby, the marquise once more fell out with chocolate.

These hesitations on the part of Madame de Sévigné testify more to the level of medical knowledge at the time, and to the purely formal terms of the debate on the effects of chocolate which enlivened aristocratic salons, rather than to a general distrust of the exotic beverage. In fact quite the opposite attitude prevailed in Europe, where, for more than half a century before Madame de Sévigné's correspondence with her daughter, the privileged circle of chocolate aficionados had never ceased to widen.

This seventeenth-century French engraving evokes all the sensual pleasures of chocolate, which were to be abundantly cultivated in the following century (above). Chocolate pots were made of earthenware, tin, tin-plated copper, silver, and sometimes even of gold. At the beginning of the eighteenth century, porcelain appeared. The chocolate pot was used both for heating and serving the beverage. Right: a Spanish porcelain chocolate pot decorated with chinoiseries (*circa* 1740).

THE EIGHTEENTH CENTURY, OR THE AGE OF DELIGHT

Numerous treatises and recipe books testify to the manner in which chocolate was prepared and consumed in Europe in the eighteenth century. In Paris, café owner Pierre Masson published a small, instructive volume in 1705 setting out the expertise required in his business. The work was called *Le Parfait Limonadier, ou la manière de préparer le thé, le café, le chocolat et autres liqueurs chaudes et froides*, and described the various ways of preparing coffee, tea, chocolate, and other beverages that his customers used to drink. His recipe for chocolate seems to reflect the most widely used method. "To make four cups of chocolate, you need four cups of water which should be heated in a chocolate pot. Take a quarter pound of chocolate, chop it as finely as possible on a sheet of paper; if you prefer it sweet, add a quarter pound of crushed sugar to the chocolate; when the water boils, plunge the whole mixture into the chocolate pot and stir it well with the chocolate stick; place it in front of the fire and when it rises, withdraw it before it boils over and beat it well with the chocolate stick to make it froth and as it does so pour it into the cups one by one; if you only want one cup, just one cupful of water is needed and one ounce of chocolate.

"And if you want to make chocolate with milk, take as much milk as you would water for proceeding as above; boil it making sure it does not turned sour and does not boil over; withdraw it from the fire and add as much sugar and chocolate as above. . . . Having poured it all into the chocolate pot, beat it well with the chocolate stick until it is frothy and serve.

"Chocolate is composed of Spanish cocoa, vanilla, cloves, cinnamon, and sugar, all of which when well prepared forms a paste which can be obtained in quarter, half, or one pound quantities, and is prepared as indicated above."

In addition to this standard preparation there were a few more sophisticated versions involving, for example, an egg yolk or a little madeira wine. In 1674 it became possible to eat chocolate in solid form, when the first eating chocolate made its appearance in London that year in "Spanish-style" sticks sold in a shop called At The Coffee Mill and Tobacco Roll. The invention met with well-deserved success and by the early eighteenth century chocolate was available all over Europe in the form of bars, tablets, and various other shapes, such as the small chocolate lozenges sometimes called *diablotins* in France.

The birth of solid chocolate heralded a new age. Gradually, helped by the profound changes which marked not only the arts, but also behavior and ideas, chocolate graduated from the status of a medicinal potion to that of a delicacy. The eighteenth

In London, chocolate-houses, unlike coffee-houses, which were serious places strictly reserved for men, enabled upper-class society to behave in an unseemly fashion in congenial company. Music, games, and flirtation offered upper-class people a more refined version of the dissolute morals which prevailed in the working-class taverns, where of course they never deigned to set foot. However, from around 1750, both chocolate- and coffee-houses disappeared one after the other, to be replaced by select clubs for gentlemen only. Only the second-rate establishments survived, frequented by the demimonde (above: a 1787 watercolor of a chocolate-house by Thomas Rowlandson).

century would abolish the social and political inertia of the previous regimes, leading to enlightened minds and more refined pleasures. On the table, light, subtle and delicately flavored dishes replaced heavy meats in strong, thick sauces. Chocolate, finally relieved of its pepper and hot spices, became the undisputed hero of the new era of culinary sensations that had dawned in Europe.

Now delicately sweetened and flavored with vanilla and cinnamon, chocolate was further exalted by a number of inspired confectioners whose sublime recipes were a delight to the palate. The days of the spicy, bitter "Indian beverage," the Spanish specialty of the previous century, were over. "Our era and the Tuscan court," wrote Italian naturalist Francesco Redi, "have added a little something of a more exquisite flavor to the Spanish perfection by adding European ingredients, such as fresh citron and lemon peel, and the subtle odor of jasmin blended with cinnamon, vanilla, ambergris and musc imparts a wonderful aroma to those who savor it." "Delectation," was the key word governing these subtle preparations. The recipe for Tuscan chocolate with a hint of jasmine, which consisted of blending cocoa with fresh jasmine according to a complex procedure, was kept secret for a long time by its creator, who worked exclusively for the Medici household. By the end of the seventeenth century, other creative geniuses invented chocolate for eating or dissolving, flavored with citrus fruit, almond paste, or flowers. However, even prepared in the standard manner, with a little sugar, vanilla, and cinnamon, chocolate was the answer to the frenzied search for pleasure and refinement which characterized the century.

At this time, chocolate was still the privilege of the wealthy few. In Mozart's opera *Così fan tutte*, the soubrette, Despina, bemoaned her lot while preparing her mistress's breakfast. "Of chocolate, I savor only the aroma. Yes fine ladies, it is you who will drink it, and I must content myself with looking at it. . . ." As to the "fine ladies," they gave themselves up to it heart and soul. Chocolate was more particularly adopted by women, who found the sweeter, more intoxicating flavors and aromas more to their liking than those of coffee. In France it was Madame de Maintenon who first persuaded her husband Louis XIV that chocolate should be served during the grand festivities in Versailles; subsequently it was used by Louis XV's court favorites, Madame de Pompadour and Madame Du Barry, each for a different purpose. The former drank chocolate perfumed with ambergris to stimulate her ardor in the company of the king, who accused her of being "as cold as a stone," the latter was said to be insatiable and to offer it to her lovers to get them in tune with her ardent temperament. Finally there was Queen Marie-Antoinette, "l'Autrichienne" (the Austrian), as she was known, who came to France to marry Louis XVI, accompanied by her

Whether in family or romantic settings, chocolate conquered the best society of the day. Facing page: *The Breakfast*, by François Boucher (1739). Above: *Madame Du Barry*, after a portrait by Greuze. This impetuous favorite of Louis XV used to ply her overworked lovers with chocolate. Subtly flavored chocolate served in fine porcelain accompanied the games of intrigue and ambition which took place in elegant salons. Right: a figurine in Meissen porcelain (1740), decorated by J.J. Kaendler. Following double page: *The Cup of Chocolate*, by Jean-Baptiste Charpentier le Vieux.

THE HISTORY OF CHOCOLATE

personal chocolate maker, a prodigious Viennese, who was expert in the art of preparing the beverage with orchid powder, orange-flower water, or milk of almonds.

The purported aphrodisiac properties of chocolate, famous since the time of the Aztecs, had never been as solicited as during the period when licentiousness was raised to the status of a lifestyle. Consequently, the chocolate ceremony was transformed into a sensual, amorous moment, propitious for seduction and particularly appreciated in boudoirs. Images of the eroticism linked with chocolate and sensual metaphors associated with the beverage abound in art and literature. The universe of the Marquis de Sade, at the extreme limit of licentious frenzy, is filled with both the amorous and fatal stimulatory properties of chocolate. "There are few games," writes Roland Barthes in *Sade, Fourier, Loyola*, "which are not assisted by a few 'stimulating comforts' such as chocolate and Spanish toasted fingers. However, on the other hand . . . stramonium is dissimulated in Minski's chocolate to send him to sleep, and poison in that of young Rose and Madame de Bressac to kill them. The Sadian chocolate, an invigorating yet murderous substance in his novels, ends up as a sign of a duplicitous nutritive economy." In a gentler vein, the typical scene depicting a lady drinking

chocolate on awakening became a classic subject in art, with the young woman still in her nightdress, revealing a charming breast or calf, languorously reclining on the rumpled sheets while the maid arrives with a steaming cup of chocolate on a tray. Moreover, sometimes the maid herself became the subject of the picture, which was the case of pretty, young Nandl Baldauf, immortalized in 1743 by a Swiss painter, Jean-Étienne Liotard. The latter had been called to Vienna to execute the portrait of the Empress Maria Theresa and her family. During his visit, Liotard was awakened every morning by a pretty chambermaid who brought him a cup of delicious hot chocolate. Charmed, he proposed that she pose with the tray in her hands. The wonderful painting resulting from this encounter, *The Beautiful Chocolate Girl*, can today be seen in the Staatliche Kunstsammlungen in Dresden. Subsequently the life of the artist's model, the chambermaid Nandl Baldauf, resembled a fairy tale, since she ended up marrying a great Viennese aristocrat, Prince Dietrichstein, and her lovely portrait by Liotard crossed the ocean to figure on packages of chocolate made by Baker, a great American manufacturer.

The attractiveness of containers is of course influenced by the value of their contents. The sensual refinement of chocolate consequently called for services of the greatest

In the eighteenth century, chocolate was still a luxury accessible only to the wealthy. However, the charming chambermaid painted by Jean-Étienne Liotard in Vienna in 1743 did end up drinking chocolate herself; Nandl Baldauf became the mistress, then the wife, of a great Austrian aristocrat (above: *The Beautiful Chocolate Girl*). Liotard painted other pictures on the same theme. In *The Breakfast* (facing page), which he painted in 1754, the chocolate is served in a beautiful Meissen porcelain cup, accompanied by a glass of water, a practice which is still fairly widespread today.

delicacy; in some cases, they were sumptuous. The essential element, the chocolate pot, invented in Spain as early as the seventeenth century, was generally wider at the base, and was equipped with a spout, and a horizontal, wooden handle. The lid had a hole in it for the whisk, which was usually made of boxwood. Sometimes the chocolate pot was mounted on a stand to accommodate a small spirit heater to be placed underneath. Standard chocolate pots were made of earthenware, tin, pewter, or tin-plated copper. However the most precious services included chocolate pots of porcelain, silver, vermeil, or even gold. The cups themselves were adapted to the new beverage. The cup as we know it with its matching saucer only appeared at the beginning of the seventeenth century. In order to be able to stir the chocolate without mishap, the *tasse trembleuse* was invented: the saucer was hollowed out in the center, and the cup was sometimes equipped with a holder to ensure stability.

Smooth, white porcelain, which so beautifully set off the deep, rich color of chocolate, reigned supreme in services in the eighteenth century. The craze for porcelain, originally imported from China, then manufactured in European factories from the first years of the century, was concomitant with the infatuation for chocolate. And so the farthest corners of east and west came to be united in European salons. Chocolate pots, porcelain cups, and small *bonbonnières*—bowls decorated with elegant floral, pastoral, or mythological motifs and filled with chocolates—set the scene perfectly for boudoir pillow talk. In some great households, the chocolate services were masterpieces of splendor and refinement created by the expert skills of the best artisans in French or German factories. Madame Du Barry's chocolate service, designed by Augustin de Saint-Aubin and made by the Sèvres porcelain factory, cost more than twenty thousand livres. Each piece was decorated with a polychrome motif of an antique-style urn overflowing with floral garlands and engraved with the monogram DB. This princely chocolate set, resplendent in its porcelain and silver finery, was only the impressive result of a long chain of labor. At the close of the century, planters, merchants, technicians, and artisans of chocolate worked behind the scenes to meet ever-increasing demand.

The Sèvres porcelain factory, established in 1756, produced magnificent chocolate services, which enhanced the color and flavor of this most intoxicating of beverages (facing page, top: chocolate cup dating from the early nineteenth century and a 1781 chocolate pot with polychrome Chinese motifs). Silversmiths also created chocolate pots in precious metals with magnificent chasing. Facing page, bottom: vermeil chocolate pot and warmer from the service which belonged to the queen of France, Marie Leszczyńska; above and left: a Sèvres porcelain chocolate service. Antique chocolate services are much sought-after by collectors.

THE FIRST FRUITS
OF AN INDUSTRY

As chocolate became increasingly popular in Europe, trade routes were developed and new trades emerged. By the end of the sixteenth century, cacao beans had begun to be imported from the American colonies for processing in Europe. During the following century, dynamic Dutch navigation companies ousted the Spaniards from their commercial supremacy. Dutch ships called at Spanish ports to unload part of their cargo before continuing along their route as far as Amster-dam, which had rapidly become the leading European port. Dutch supremacy was overwhelming during the first quarter of the seventeenth century; not one single cargo of American cacao was loaded onto a Spanish vessel in this period.

Succeeding the monasteries and convents, the first chocolate factories made their appearance in Europe in the middle of the seventeenth century. In these pioneering establishments, chocolate production was archaic and still inspired by primitive Mexican techniques. The worker, kneeling in front of a heated, tilted stone, ground the beans by

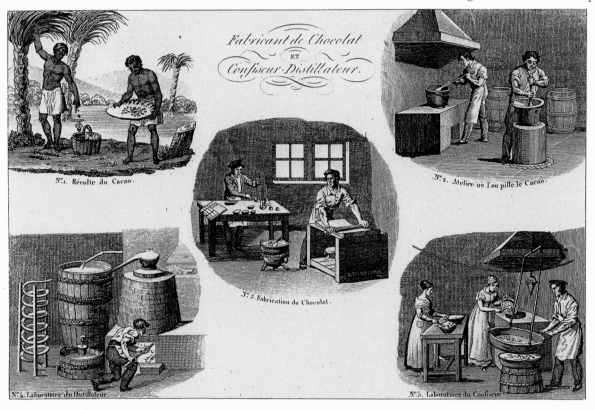

The first technical advances in chocolate manufacturing only appeared in the 1770s, with the arrival of "industrial" chocolate. Up until then, the whole process had been carried out entirely by hand. The only noteworthy advance prior to that date, invented by a Frenchman named Dubuisson in 1732, was the charcoal-fired horizontal grinding table, which enabled the workers to grind the beans standing up. It can be seen in this nineteenth-century engraving from the *Galerie industrielle*, which illustrates the various phases of chocolate manufacture.

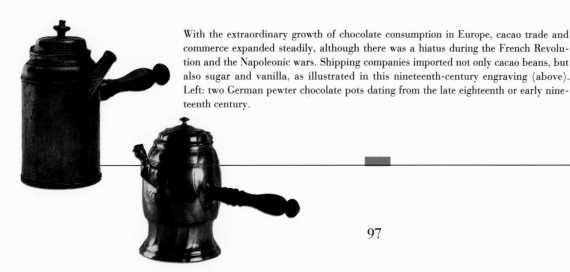

hand with an iron cylinder. However, the first technical advances were soon developed. In France, in 1732, a certain Monsieur Dubuisson invented a horizontal table heated by charcoal, which enabled the grinder to work more efficiently in a standing position. Four years prior to Dubuisson's invention, another technical advance appeared in Great Britain in the form of a hydraulic press, which was installed by Walter Churchman, a manufacturer in Bristol. However, the change to mechanized processes was slow, and in France the first hydraulic grinding machine did not come into use until 1778. This major invention, which was the work of a certain Monsieur Doret, coincided with the appearance of the first industrial chocolate companies which sold their products through a network of grocery or confectionery retailers. The soon-to-be-famous Compagnie Française des Chocolats et Thés Pelletier & Cie., a chocolate and tea company, was founded in Paris in 1770, and La Chocolaterie Royale Le Grand d'Aussy was established in 1776. The chocolate factories in Bayonne, which had become France's main production center following the introduction of the new beverage by the marranos (Spanish Jews driven out of Spain in the sixteenth century), were equipped with steam-driven machines in 1780.

Competition grew and commercial techniques were developed. In 1776, the Parisian tradesman, Monsieur Roussel, put an advertisement in the Mercure de France. "Monsieur Roussel, grocer in the Saint-Germain-des-Près

Abbey, deeming that the use of chocolate is becoming widespread, as much for health as for pleasure . . . informs the public, as a citizen desirous of being useful to his compatriots, and to avoid any unpleasant surprises, that every block of chocolate leaving his factory will be imprinted with his name and residence."

The American War of Independence, the French Revolution, and the Napoleonic wars in Europe curbed chocolate production and consumption, bringing the product practically to a standstill for the duration of the Continental System, an economic blockade Napoleon tried to enforce against Great Britain from 1806. Four years earlier, the first gastronomic guide, *l'Almanach des gourmands*, by Grimod de la Reynière, was published in Paris. The first volume of the work, entitled *Itinéraire nutritif*, took its readers on a gastronomic tour of Paris, where the upheavals of history had not yet made chocolate prices prohibitive. "At no. 41 [on the rue Vivienne], we enter Monsieur Lemoine's superb boutique, where we are struck by his ingenious display of liqueurs, chocolates and sweets. . . . The eminently creamy quality of his chocolate is due to the new methods Monsieur Lemoine employs in cacao grinding. He owes his well-founded, brilliant reputation to the combination of two products, liqueurs and chocolate, both so important to gourmets, and he spares no effort to live up to it." Grimod de La Reynière also recommended "one of the best confectioners in Paris," Tanrade, on the rue Neuve-Le Pelletier, and his "exquisite

With the extraordinary growth of chocolate consumption in Europe, cacao trade and commerce expanded steadily, although there was a hiatus during the French Revolution and the Napoleonic wars. Shipping companies imported not only cacao beans, but also sugar and vanilla, as illustrated in this nineteenth-century engraving (above). Left: two German pewter chocolate pots dating from the late eighteenth or early nineteenth century.

AIMEZ - VOUS LE CHOCOLAT, MONSIEUR LE DUC ?

En 1807 l'Empereur à Dantzig voulant récompenser le M.ᵈˡ Lefevre pour sa conquête de cette ville, le fit inviter à déjeuner. le Maréchal arrivé Bonjour M.ʳ le Duc lui dit Napoléon, & M.ᵈᵉ étonné crut que sa majesté plaisantait l'Empereur ajouta Aimez-vous le chocolat? Mais oui sir et bien je vais vous en donner une livre de la ville de Dantzig. l'Empereur se leva & offrit au Maréchal une sorte de tablette lui disant Duc de Dantzig acceptez ce chocolat les petits cadeaux entretiennent l'amitié. Le duc ouvrant chez lui ces tablettes vit que c'était un présent mille écus en billets de banque et un duché pour le prix d'une citadelle.

chocolate, prepared with cacao chosen with extraordinary care." On the Grands Boulevards, Tortoni's chocolate seemed to him "almost as good as that of the king of Spain." The chocolate itinerary also led to the rue Saint-Dominique, where Grimod recommended Debauve, a celebrated chocolate firm which still exists today. "We cannot examine in this volume all the chocolates that this skillful artisan concocts, for he employs Spanish, Piedmontese, and Italian methods, as though Madrid, Florence, Genoa, and Turin were teamed up in his boutique and were vying with Bayonne for the supreme honor. We will only mention his analeptic chocolate, made with salep . . ." Grimod also detailed the therapeutic properties of this substance, which is extracted from a certain orchid tuber.

Napoleon reputedly always carried chocolate during his campaigns, and for the Spanish guerrillas who valiantly resisted him it is said to have been practically their sole source of nourishment. The defenders of the town of Danzig, who surrendered to Marshal Lefebvre in 1807, would perhaps have been well advised to have followed their example. As a reward, the emperor dubbed Lefebvre duke in an amusing little ceremony, during which chocolate was served (above: an engraving from 1834 illustrating the scene). Right: an early nineteenth-century German porcelain *trembleuse* cup.

As the Continental System continued, Grimod de La Reynière noted in the 1808 edition of his *Almanach*, "the fantastic rise in price of sugar and cacao." The shortage caused prices to soar, which discouraged consumers. A large number of chocolate manufacturers had to close down, while others only managed to survive by resorting to dubious methods. "There are some chocolates in Paris which contain anything except cacao. . . . Substances are introduced which could seriously incommode those who consume them, such as inferior brown sugar, flour, and even starch, which constitutes a serious and punishable offense." These reprehensible methods testified to the constant and pressing demand for chocolate on the part of frustrated consumers. Never had the chocolate mania been more pathetic than during those times of shortage.

The return of peace in 1815 marked a veritable renaissance. People's love of chocolate was undiminished, the grinding and pressing machines had not rusted, and the expertise of chocolate makers was still intact. When the supply of cacao beans was restored, the much awaited recovery in this dormant sector was immediate.

The industrial revolution brought important transformations, and the 1820s marked the beginning of chocolate for all. A flourishing industry backed by considerable technical progress was to make the "food of the gods" into an everyday, universal delicacy available to all. This opened a new chapter in the history of chocolate, now a popular, mass-produced product, whose first heroes were named Van Houten, Menier, Suchard, and Kohler. This chapter, for the greater joy of all of us, is still far from finished.

"Such are Monsieur Debauve's chocolates: they owe their supremacy to a good choice of raw materials, to the firm pledge that nothing inferior will leave his factory, and to the expert eye of the master who supervises all the details of manufacture." The Debauve establishment, extolled here by Brillat-Savarin in his work *Physiologie du gout*, was founded in 1800. It still exists today housed in a magnificent building (classed as a historic national monument) reminiscent of a small ancient temple, complete with wooden counter and imitation marble pillars.

GREAT
NAMES
IN
CHOCOLATE

FRENCH
CHOCOLATE
Maîtres Chocolatiers

"At my father's house, we used to make our own chocolate; chocolate in those days was made from cocoa powder, sugar, and vanilla. The damp, soggy bricks of chocolate were put out to dry on the terrace at the top of the house. And every morning, the surface of the chocolate revealed, in the form of hollow, five-petaled flowers, the nocturnal wanderings of our cats." (Colette, *La Maison de Claudine*).

By the end of the nineteenth century, France could boast a veritable army of chocolate "makers." The dynamism of the pioneering chocolate industrialists like Poulain, Menier, and Barry in no way hindered the development of small, independently owned, artisanal chocolate firms, which flourished until the end of the Second World War. At the beginning of the nineteenth century, apothecaries ground cacao beans to make chocolate and, in order to enhance its virtues, they incorporated a variety of often astonishing ingredients. The celebrated firm of Debauve & Gallais, founded in 1800 and today the oldest makers of handmade chocolate in Paris, admittedly no longer produces "medicinal" chocolates, such as "analeptic" chocolate made with "Persian tonic," Indian tapioca "pectoral" chocolate, "very useful for persons with chest conditions," or chocolate tonic with Japanese cashew extract.

One of France's most celebrated *maîtres chocolatiers*, Maurice Bernachon of Lyon personally selects the cacao beans that will go into his secret blends of "grand cru" chocolates (page 104). Across the Alps, in Turin, the venerable Peyrano firm still makes its renowned gianduiotti according to time-honored, artisanal traditions (page 105). On the boulevard Saint-Germain-des-Prés in the heart of Paris, the Debauve & Gallais store, which dates from 1819, still has the delightfully old-fashioned charm of a nineteenth-century apothecary shop (above). Posters by artists, including the celebrated Czech Art Nouveau painter and designer Alphonse Mucha (1860–1939), have contributed to the popular imagery associated with chocolate.

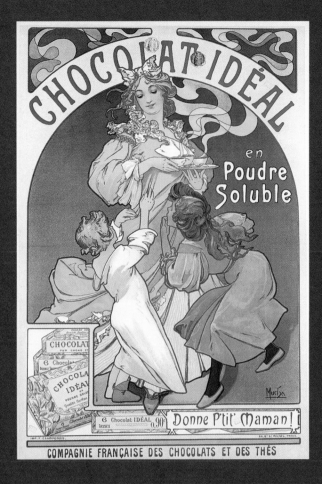

However, Debauve & Gallais still sells a range of historical chocolates, including "les pistoles de Marie-Antoinette," made with almond milk or orange-flower water, and their famous unsweetened health chocolate.

SAVOIR-FAIRE

Today, fewer than ten French chocolate manufacturers still begin with the raw cacao beans to make their chocolate. One such firm—based in Lyon—is run by Maurice Bernachon, who, along with his son Jean-Jacques, roasts his own carefully selected beans from the Indian Ocean, South America, and Indonesia. The beans are combined in different proportions to create a dozen "crus," whose jealously guarded secret recipes were perfected by Maurice Bernachon during the 1970s. "At that time, it seemed to me that we were heading toward a standardization of taste, so I began to combine different varieties of cacao beans and torrefy them myself to create a unique chocolate with a distinctive flavor." Motivated by the same desire to escape conformity, Raymond Bonnat, based in Voiron in the Isère region near Grenoble, and, more recently, François Pralus in the Loire Valley also began to roast their own cacao beans.

Like wine connoisseurs, chocolate specialists can identify specific *terroirs*, or soils, within each cacao-producing country. "Unfortunately," explains Jérôme Garret, a buyer

for the Bordeaux-based Touton firm which supplies beans to chocolate manufacturers, "the diversity of the cacao beans available on the world market is diminishing because traditional cacao trees like the criollo are fragile and are being replaced increasingly by more hardy and profitable hybrids." At Valrhona, based in Tain-l'Hermitage in the Drôme region, the quality of each cacao-bean shipment is tested by a panel of ten experts who meet every two weeks. The "noses," to borrow a term from perfume-making, are asked to establish the "aromatic profile" of the beans. They evaluate the beans based on twenty precise criteria, among which are acidity, bitterness, notes of caramel, dried fruits or red berry fruits, or a grilled or burned aroma. The result is a veritable "cacao-bean library," which records the history of the firm's imports and forms a valuable quality-control tool.

According to Robert Linxe, the founder of the Maison du Chocolat in Paris, "The flavor of a well-made chocolate should develop progressively on the palate." In formulating the optimal combination of flavors, the chocolate maker must provide for "head notes" (the initial taste) and "heart notes" (the subtle undertones) as well as the persistence of the taste after the chocolate has been eaten. Just the right balance must be struck between the smooth, slightly bitter flavor of Chuao cacao beans from Venezuela (the most highly prized), the admirably long-lasting savor of the Porto Cabello bean (also from Venezuela), the sensual

Valrhona, based in Tain-l'Hermitage, a small town in the Rhône valley, is a leading supplier of couverture chocolates for small manufacturers. The carefully selected cacao beans are roasted during the torrefaction process (facing page, top). Almonds or hazelnuts are slowly coated with chocolate in these copper revolving pens, and then "polished" to give them a glossy finish (facing page, bottom). Jean-Jacques Bernachon is about to test the flavor of a truffle, one of the Bernachon specialties. The sack on the counter contains grand cru Venezuelan cacao beans, and on the wall behind hangs an array of heavy copper basins used in the preparation of praline and ganache fillings (above).

strength of Madagascar beans, and the Sri Lanka bean, which, though deliciously perfumed, lacks body. The chocolate produced by Weiss, a manufacturer based in Saint-Étienne since 1882, has a unique flavor due to the blending of Sambirano beans from Madagascar, Santa Severa beans from Trinidad, Carenero beans from Venezuela, and Arriba beans from Ecuador.

The opposite approach was taken by Raymond Bonnat, whose objective was to emphasize the origins of the beans, much as wine-makers do with grapes. This led him to develop the seven "crus," each composed of one variety of bean, which go into his basic recipe for dark chocolate. The infinitely subtle and aromatic flavor of the trinitario bean contrasts with that of the Maragnan bean, a Venezuelan variety which sometimes produces extraordinary harvests, or with the delicate Sri Lanka bean, which is pale in color with orange highlights. In fact, the color of the beans varies as much as their flavor, ranging from dark brown to beige with shades of ochre or purple, chestnut or violet. "The best chocolate is not black," explains Robert Linxe, "too dark a color always denotes beans of mediocre origin." This observation is echoed by the Parisian chocolatier, Christian Constant, who adds, "A good chocolate has mahogany-colored highlights."

Each type of cacao bean necessitates a different degree of torrefaction and is therefore roasted separately. At regular intervals, a small quantity of beans are removed and examined. As Jean-Jacques Bernachon remarks, "Sight and smell are more reliable guides than the automatic timer!" When split in half, the burning-hot bean should reveal purplish glints and smell strongly of cocoa. When this occurs, the beans are roasted to perfection. The torrefaction process is immediately halted and the are beans left to cool. They are then put into a winnowing machine which, by a system of ventilation and sieves, removes the outer husks, leaving behind small kernels, known as nibs, which are the heart of the cacao bean. At Bonnat, the hundred-year-old winnowing machine made of exotic wood is still in use. Despite a certain bitterness, the nibs already have an aroma of chocolate. Some chocolate makers even use them in this state, "which preserves the original, raw flavor of the cacao bean," explains Pierre Hermé, the pastry chef at Fauchon in Paris, who uses the roasted nibs in an ultra-fine nougatine. Michel Chaudun used nibs instead of ground almonds or hazelnuts in the dark chocolate "cacao bean chip" bar he created for Weiss.

After being reduced to nibs, cacao beans are still only at the beginning of the process which will transform them into chocolate; the master chocolatier has yet to perform the necessary alchemy to release their hidden savors. First, different varieties of nibs are assembled depending on the manufacturer's requirements. They are then passed through granite rollers which grind them into a thick, aromatic paste, known as the

The pride and joy of the Bonnat firm, this century-old winnowing machine made of exotic wood is used to clean and sort the roasted cacao beans and to remove their husks (above). Master chocolate maker Raymond Bonnat is a purist; he believes that a single, excellent "grand cru" bean is the key to producing a peerless chocolate. In contrast, Weiss, the prestigious chocolate manufacturer based in Saint-Étienne for over a century, offers a symphony of flavors resulting from constant experimentation and the blending of cacao beans of widely diverse origins (facing page).

chocolate liquor, or mass. To produce cocoa powder, the chocolate liquor is transferred to a hydraulic press which extracts the cocoa butter and leaves behind a dry residue, known as the "cake," which is the basic ingredient of cocoa powder. Chocolate liquor destined for use in eating chocolate will not pass through a press; rather, it will go into a mixer where it is ground and pulverised further, becoming increasingly smooth. The heat generated by this operation melts the cocoa butter and liquifies the chocolate paste; it is at this stage that granulated sugar is added. "Like salt, sugar greatly intensifies flavor. Too little is just as harmful as too much," underlines Michel Richard, a chocolate maker in Lyon, who signs his creations "Richart." The mixture is then kneaded and ground once again until no particles are discernible to the palate, and extra cocoa butter is sometimes added to increase malleability. The refining process is continued in conching machines, which are large, heated vats in which the sweetened chocolate is constantly mixed and aerated. The chocolate is now at its best, its texture creamy and its aroma and flavor fully developed. Côte de France, a factory founded in 1936 at Vitry, manufactures chocolate which is renowned for its smoothness. "This is because we conch for ten days and nights," explains the company director, Philippe Wasterlain, "which economically speaking is absolutely unreasonable, but

which results in the remarkable creaminess we achieve."

The chocolate still has to undergo the tempering process, which not only enables the finished chocolate to break cleanly, but also gives it a beautiful sheen. In concrete terms, the chocolate is melted at a temperature of approximately 120°F, is then cooled to about 85°F and reheated slightly—the temperatures vary depending on the type of chocolate. According to scientists, this provokes very fine crystallization of the cocoa butter. The chocolate is now ready to be molded into candy bars, hearts for Valentine's Day, eggs and rabbits for Easter, Santa Claus and his reindeer for Christmas, and square "neapolitans" for serving with coffee (a Weiss specialty since the 1920s). It is also ready to fill the interior of plain chocolate eggshells for Bonnat, or to coat crystallized ginger, candied orange peel, caramelized almonds, or real arabica coffee beans for Debauve & Gallais. To obtain milk chocolate, condensed milk or milk crumb is added to the chocolate liquor at the same time as the sugar. Some types of cacao bean are preferred for use in milk chocolate, the Java bean, for example, which is pale in color and has a natural, faint caramel flavor which blends perfectly with milk.

SUBTLE GANACHE

The work of the chocolate maker is not limited to producing chocolate from raw materials. In fact, the majority subcontract this operation out to specialized firms which process the beans according to the specific instructions of each customer. These suppliers range from large corporations like Cacao Barry, to smaller establishments such

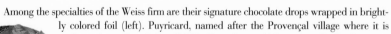

Among the specialties of the Weiss firm are their signature chocolate drops wrapped in brightly colored foil (left). Puyricard, named after the Provençal village where it is located, was founded in 1967 by Jean-Guy and Marie-Anne Roelandt, a couple of Belgian origin. They make luxurious chocolates in the Belgian tradition, but add their own touch by using French regional products such as fresh cream from Brittany or milk from Normandy. After enchanting chocolate lovers in the south of France for almost thirty years, Puyricard has now opened shops in Paris and in Canada (facing page).

as Valrhona in the Drôme, Weiss in Saint-Éti-enne, or the very modest Chocolaterie du Pecq near Paris, which produces approximately twenty-five kinds of high-quality couverture chocolate. These include the dark chocolate Guanaja, Manjari or Pur Caraïbe couvertures, made from Caribbean cacao beans which imbue the chocolate with a warm, sensual, almost woody flavor; or milk chocolate varieties such as Jivara, which has delicate notes of caramel and vanilla. The master chocolatier will use these couverture chocolates to make handmade palets d'or, truffles, liqueur chocolates, or pralines.

According to Robert Linxe, "Of all the available chocolate fillings, ganache is certainly the most interesting, because it is the one that requires the highest percentage of cocoa solids." Making a successful ganache involves skill and a great deal of inspiration. First, the ganache cream must be brought to a boil. Then the couverture chocolate is grated with a knife and added to the cream. The dark shavings melt and blend into the white liquid. The mixture thickens and gradually becomes completely homogenous, while a strong, delicious aroma of chocolate pervades the air, sharpened by the slightly acrid odor of the cream. A natural ganache made in this way will have a high cocoa content and is used to make palets d'or, a confection invented by Bernard Sérardy in Moulins in 1898 and revived in this century by Maurice Bernachon.

In formulating a ganache filling, the chocolate maker may indulge in any flight of fancy as long as it tastes good. For example, the fresh cream may be flavored by infusing it with roasted coffee beans or vanilla pods, jasmine flowers, Chinese tea leaves, Java pepper, or liquorice. Christian Constant flavors his ganache with exotic ingredients like cinnamon, cloves, curcuma, safran, cardamom, or vervain, whose only function is to "liberate the savor already present in chocolate." Robert Linxe also makes sure that his chocolate has a flavor that is is as distinctive as possible. One of his latest creations, a wild-peach-flavored ganache, achieves a perfect and original harmony between the acidity of the fruit and the intense flavors of the dark chocolate. Another of his ganache specialties, the lemon-flavored Andalousie, requires the patience of a saint to make because the lemon peel has to be rubbed with pieces of sugar. "The zest by itself is too bitter," explains Robert Linxe, who is known to admirers as "the magician of ganache." For Bernard Dufoux, the only way to obtain a real raspberry, fresh mint, or blackberry

flavor is to boil the cream with raspberry, mint, or bramble leaves from his garden. "They should be picked before the buds appear," he specifies, "otherwise they lose their flavor."

No task is too difficult if it brings the chocolate closer to perfection. Fillings for assorted chocolates present limitless possibilities and most artisanal chocolate makers offer several dozen varieties, which at their best have a superb, velvety consistency and incomparable flavor.

Natural vanilla comes tied in bunches measuring 5½ to 8 inches (above). Known to the Aztecs as early as A.D. 1000, vanilla pods are the dried fruit of a variety of climbing orchid whose large white or yellow flowers bloom for only one day. In the eighteenth century, Brillat-Savarin praised the incomparable taste of chocolate which has been flavored with vanilla. Chocolate has played a significant role in the history of pastry. Since the seventeenth century, its endless possibilities have allowed a small number of inspired pastry chefs to become legendary. Fortunes have been made, dynasties founded, and empires built on the basis of their recipes (facing page).

POULAIN AND MENIER: THE GREAT INDUSTRIALISTS

Chocolate connoisseurs are all familiar with the master chocolatiers who use only the best ingredients to produce fine, handmade chocolate. However, it was enterprising industrialists who, during the nineteenth century, brought this delicious commodity within the reach of people of more modest means. Many of these famous brands, such as Poulain, Menier, and more recently, Barry, continue to sell fine, mass-produced chocolate today.

Victor-Auguste Poulain's parents were farmers in the Loir-et-Cher *département* in central France. The youngest of a large family, he was considered too weak to work in the fields and was left home at the age of ten with ten *sous* in his pocket. He found employment as an apprentice with various local grocery stores and, when he was a bit older, moved to Paris, where he was hired as an assistant at the Mortier d'Argent, a well-known purveyor of comestibles on rue Monsieur-le-Prince. The owner made his own chocolate, which he sold, in between the sugar loaves, wrapped in their traditional blue paper, the bottles of ratafia, anisette, and muscatel, and the barrels of molasses. Auguste, as he was called, spent nearly a decade there, learning the trade and saving every penny. At the age of twenty-two, with thirteen years of solid experience behind him and a small nest egg of eighteen hundred francs, he decided to return home to the Loire region, settling in Blois in 1847. There were already five well-established chocolate manufacturers in town, but this did not deter the young man from opening his own shop in 1848, or from marrying in the same year.

All the chocolate sold by Auguste Poulain was made entirely by hand in the back of his shop. Poulain understood the importance of offering his customers a "loyal" chocolate, by which he meant inexpensive but of honest, reliable quality. The Poulains had to sell their personal belongings more than once to buy and equip new workshops, and finally were able to build a small factory. In 1867 the firm opened a warehouse in Paris on rue Neuve-des-Petits-Champs. Around this time, Auguste Poulain, sporting his ubiquitous black silk skullcap, came up with the firm's celebrated slogan, *"Goûtez et comparez"* (taste and compare). It would seem that the French "tasted and compared" a great deal, because by 1878 the Poulain factories were producing approximately five tons of chocolate per day. At this point Auguste's son, Albert, went into business with his father, but the company philosophy remained the same: *"vendre bon et à bon marché"* (sell good quality at good prices). In 1884, Albert Poulain introduced a new product which was to revolutionize the eating habits of millions of French children. This was a vanilla-flavored, chocolate breakfast drink mix called Petit Déjeuner à la Crème Vanillée, which sold for five centimes a tin. It was the precurser of the Pulvérisé drink mix, known as Poulain Orange, launched in 1904, which the French continue to buy today under its modern appellation of Grand Arôme. Searching for ideas to increase sales of his new invention, Albert Poulain had a

Poulain Orange instant cocoa powder—the forerunner of France's current favorite, Grand Arôme—received a dynamic, modern image in 1920 in this poster designed by the Italian graphic artist Leonetto Capiello, which won over generations of French consumers (left). Beginning in 1904, each tin of Poulain Orange contained a small metal figurine and a color picture-card, destined to increase the impact of the famous slogan *"Goûtez et comparez"* (taste and compare) and to build brand loyalty, particularly among children, who were the main consumers of the product. Poulain was the first to use this inspired advertising strategy, which was immensely successful and widely imitated (right and facing page).

brainstorm: he decided to include a small metal figurine and a color picture-card in each tin. The success of this clever sales ploy was immediate and soon dozens of other chocolate manufacturers followed suit.

Another great French industrial chocolate fortune, that of the Menier family, also had its roots in the first half of the nineteenth century. Jean-Antoine Brutus Menier, a pharmacist, was moderately renowned for the quality of his "impalpable medicinal powders," which he manufactured in Paris using horse-driven mills. Hearing that a water mill was for rent on the banks of the river Marne in Noisiel, he did not hesitate to take out a lease on it and was soon grinding his pharmaceutical preparations less expensively and more efficiently through water power. He subsequently bought the mill, along with the approximately thirty-seven hundred acres of land surrounding it. Not long afterwards, Menier decided to purchase a small chocolate factory in the vicinity; he

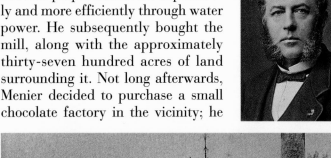

thought that chocolate could turn out to be useful, perhaps for coating pills. The Menier empire began to grow, though at Jean-Antoine's death, in 1853, the Noisiel plant was only producing a few thousand tons of chocolate a year compared to two hundred thousand tons of medicinal powders.

When Jean-Antoine's son, Émile-Justin, also a pharmacist, took over the firm at the age of twenty-seven, he decided to concentrate on chocolate manufacture. In 1867, this ardent idealist embarked on an unprecedented adventure, which combined the building of an industrial enterprise with an enlightened vision of capitalism. Esteeming that his company would be more profitable if it controled the entire chocolate-production chain, Émile Menier bought cacao plantations in Nicaragua, acquired considerable stock in sugar refineries, purchased a flotilla of ships, and even planted poplar groves on the banks of the Marne to supply the wood used to

When the young pharmacist Émile-Justin Menier (above, top) succeeded his father Jean-Antoine, he abandoned "medicinal powders" in favor of chocolate production. Under the leadership of this enlightened industrialist, the company became the leading chocolate manufacturer in the world. This general view shows the Menier plant at Noisiel in *circa* 1900 (above). The Menier factory, built by Saulnier in 1869, a masterpiece of industrial architecture and, classified as a national historical monument, today belongs to Nestlé-France (facing page).

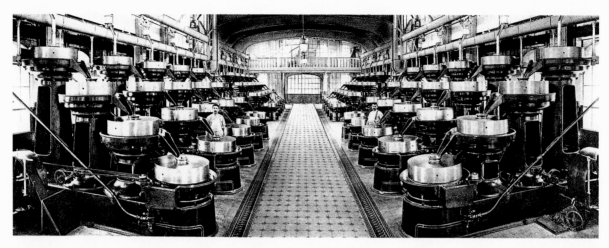

make the Menier delivery crates. In 1870, he opened a factory in London and a warehouse in New York. However, for Émile Menier, his most important accomplishment came in 1874, when he constructed a village composed of individual houses with gardens to lodge the *"chocolats"* as the chocolate factory employees were called. This "ville Menier," which inspired the setting for Hector Malot's novel, *En Famille*, offered extraordinary amenities for the period, including free education and healthcare, and a library. Similar model villages would be built by the Cadbury brothers in England (1879) and by Milton Hershey in the United States (1906). Émile Menier was a generous patron whose profound interest in industry inspired him to invest in both rubber and electric cables. He was a free-thinker and staunch republican, and when

elected to represent the Seine-et-Marne *département* at the Assemblée Nationale, he advocated the application of a capital gains tax. Following Émile Menier's death in 1881 at the age of fifty-five, his son Henri inherited the company. Continuing his father's good works, Henri Menier had electricity and telephones installed in the workers' homes in 1889 and two years later, eighty-two years before the rest of the active population in France, Menier employees were accorded the right to retire at the age of sixty.

Production expanded rapidly and by 1867 Menier was producing a spectacular 25,000 tons of chocolate a year, which propelled it to the forefront of the French chocolate industry. At consecutive World's Fairs, Menier chocolates won medal after medal. For French children, Menier's success meant

Production at the Menier factory was completely automated by the beginning of the twentieth century, which allowed the manufacture of chocolate bars untouched by human hands, reflecting the firm's concern for quality and hygiene (top). The slogan immortalized in this poster, created by the painter Firmin Bouisset in 1893, translates as "Don't accept imitation brands" (above). The Menier empire stretched all the way to Nicaragua, where Émile-Justin Menier had purchased a cacao plantation to ensure a regular arrival of high-quality raw materials (facing page, top). This engraving of the Noisiel factory by Poyet appeared in the catalogue of the 1900 World's Fair (facing page, bottom).

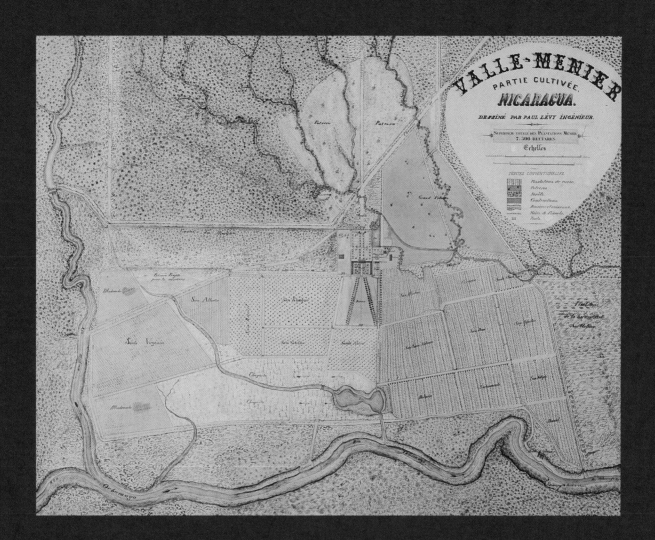

chocolate bars to accompany their afternoon snacks of bread and butter. A famous advertising poster, created in 1891 by Firmin Bouisset, shows a little girl with braids writing the name Menier on the wall. Indulgence in chocolate had become a delightful vice shared by all.

Today, Poulain and Menier are no longer independent companies, rather they are brand names owned by multinational corporations. Poulain was bought out by Cadbury-Schweppes, and the Menier saga came to an end in 1959. Nestlé-France now owns the Noisiel plant—several buildings of which are classified as national historical landmarks—where it plans to transfer its corporate headquarters. Today, the Menier name appears only on the green-paper wrappers of one type of dark baking chocolate, along with pictures of the gold medals it won so long ago.

The Charles Barry chocolate company, founded in 1842 by the Englishman after whom it is named, did not have production facilities in France until the turn of the twentieth century, when it opened a factory at Meulan. Like Poulain and Menier, Charles Barry produced pure, plain chocolate sold by grocery stores. However, the product that made the company famous was its celebrated cocoa powder, known as Cacao Barry. In 1952, company policy changed and the directors of the firm decided to concentrate exclusively on cacao bean processing in order to supply industrial and artisanal chocolate makers with the basic ingredients required for the production of chocolate bars, candies, ice cream, or pastries. As the twentieth century draws to a close, the general trend has been for more and more specialization at each stage of chocolate manufacture. Barry is now France's leading cacao bean processor, and its fourteen factories throughout the world testify to the company's international expansion. Some 170,000 tons of roasted beans are ground annually at the group's extensive production facilities in Louviers, Cameroon, and the Ivory Coast, while at the new Meulan factory, technicians work minor miracles in the field of physical chemistry in order to meet the increasingly specialized demands of their customers.

Finally, a modern chocolate success story deserves mention. In 1962 Georges Poirrier, an industrialist from Perpignan in southwestern France, took over a small chocolate factory located in the nearby community of Arles-sur-Tech. Founded by Parès and run by his decendant, Léon Cantalou, the factory's output at the time of the takeover hardly exceeded 4 to 5 tons per day. Today, Cantalou ranks among the leading chocolate manufacturers in France and is the owner of the world's largest molding machine, which has a production capacity of sixty thousand chocolate bars per hour. In other words, one chocolate bar in three sold in France today, irrespective of the brand, is manufactured at the Cantalou factories. Chocolate has entered the age of high technology.

The British chocolate maker Charles Barry, based in France since the beginning of the twentieth century, met with instant success when he introduced his famous tins of Cacao Barry (above). In 1926, Moupot's poster for the Cémoi brand of chocolate deliberately abandoned the world of childhood to address, openly and elegantly, the female consumer, who, as everyone knows, adores chocolate (facing page).

SWISS CHOCOLATE

Milk Chocolate and Fondant

Switzerland has made two towering contributions to worldwide chocolate production: the fortuitous invention of milk chocolate; and the development of creamy fondant chocolate, which is the basic ingredient of innumerable chocolate products. Chocolate arrived in Switzerland in the 1750s, sold by traveling Italian merchants, known as *cioccolatieri*. The chocolate they sold at fairs and markets was made in the form of long rolls, which were sliced by weight. However, the history of Swiss chocolate as we know it today did not truly begin until the nineteenth century, with the advent of Switzerland's celebrated chocolate pioneers, Cailler, Kohler, Peter, Suchard, Tobler, Nestlé, and Lindt.

François-Louis Cailler opened the first chocolate factory in Switzerland in 1819 at Corsier, not far from Vevey, following a four-year apprenticeship with the celebrated Italian chocolate firm Caffarel. In Italy Cailler had observed the laborious grinding of cacao beans and sugar, and in order to improve the process for his own factory, he designed a small water mill equipped with two granite millstones which revolved at the same speed and were powered by a nearby stream. His specialties, "pur caraque" and "commun sucré," blends of cocoa paste, vanilla, and cinnamon, were sold to a local clientele. Motivated by Cailler's success, Amédée Kohler, the owner of a colonial commodities trading company since 1818, embarked on his own chocolate venture in 1830. In order to create an original product, he added hazelnuts to his chocolate paste.

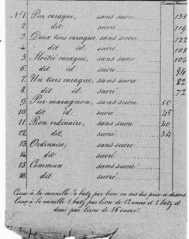

MILK AND CHOCOLATE

During this period, chocolate makers all over Europe were striving to develop a successful combination of chocolate and milk. Swiss chocolate makers were among the leaders of this effort. It was around this time, in 1863, that Daniel Peter, a candle-maker's apprentice in Vevey, married Cailler's daughter. Becoming a chocolate maker by marriage, he manufactured

The first Swiss-made chocolates were manufactured at François-Louis Cailler's factory near Vevey, opened in 1819 (above). The Suchard chocolate empire has its roots in Philipp Suchard's first shop in Neuchâtel, where he sold fine chocolates, including his famous "diablotins," which were to captivate the world (facing page, top). In 1875, Daniel Peter, François-Louis Cailler's son-in-law, invented milk chocolate by adding Nestlé's powdered milk to cocoa paste. This poster for Peter's Original Milk-Chocolate dates from 1920 (facing page, middle). Amédée Kohler designed striking packaging with an Art Nouveau flavor for his celebrated hazelnut chocolate (facing page, bottom).

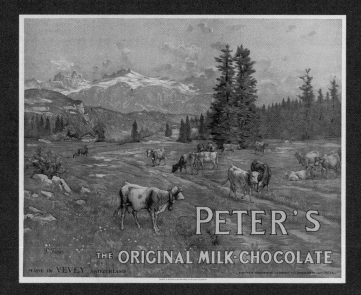

standard chocolate during the day and spent his evenings in search of a formula to combine milk with cocoa powder. The task was made all the more difficult by the high-humidity content of whole milk, which destroyed the texture of the chocolate. Breakthroughs in the area of food conservation held great promise, particularly the condensed milk developed during the 1850s in the United States, and Henri Nestlé 's powdered milk. Peter hoped that the new condensed milk process would provide the solution to his problem. Success came in 1875, when Peter discovered the key to uniting milk and chocolate, and created a milk chocolate recipe that has never been equaled.

In 1904, Henri Nestlé decided to branch out into chocolate production. He acquired a controlling interest in the Société Suisse de Chocolats, a company which already grouped the Peter and Kohler firms. In 1911, the firm of Alexandre Cailler, the grandson of François-Louis Cailler, also became part of the group. Today, the Nestlé corporation still manufactures products originally created by Cailler, Kohler, and Peter. Three products are especially popular: Cailler milk chocolate, which connoisseurs immediately recognize by its pronounced milky, "barnyard" flavor (a description which, in fact, has nothing derogatory about it), dark chocolate or Crémant, and Nestlé milk chocolate, based on Daniel Peter's original recipe.

THE SUCHARD ODYSSEY

The fine reputation of Swiss chocolate owes much to the Suchard family. Philipp Suchard's interest in chocolate began in 1809, when the young boy went to the apothecary's to buy a pound of chocolate for his ailing mother and was shocked to discover that it cost the equivalent of three days of wages for a workman. He soon left home to take up an apprenticeship with his brother, who was a confectioner in Bern. In 1825, Philipp Suchard opened his own confectionery shop in Neuchâtel, only to move to Serrières the following year. True success came with his introduction of chocolate lozenges known as "diablotins," which caused a veritable sensation. The firm expanded rapidly. At the Great Exhibition of 1851 in London, and the 1855 Exposition Universelle held in Paris, Suchard chocolates won all the gold medals available for a food product. Following the death of Philipp Suchard, his son traveled the world to expand the family business. After his premature death, his brother-in-law, Carl Russ, took over the firm. In 1901, he oversaw the production of Suchard's first milk chocolate bar, the famous Milka. However, Suchard enthusiasts saw the flavor of their favorite chocolate

This delightfully impish poster from *circa* 1900 reflects the charming, child-oriented image Suchard projected through advertising and packaging (top). A happy little girl waves from this cardboard display, which was used in retail stores selling Suchard products (left). An idyllic scene typical of the year 1900 decorates a box of assorted Suchard chocolates (right). In this beautiful 1890 poster for Suchard cocoa, the young apprentice with a basket full of treats on his head seems blissfully unaware that he is spilling fragrant chocolate along the way (facing page).

tainted with bitterness when Carl Russ's successor, Willy Russ, sold his shares to the French Poulain chocolate company in 1930. When the American multinational Philip Morris bought out Suchard in 1990 and moved the production facilities from Serrières to a modern plant near Bern, the transfomation of the venerable Swiss firm was complete. Though the quality of the chocolate is unchanged, the taste has never been quite the same.

FONDANT CHOCOLATE

In 1879 Rodolphe Lindt invented the conching machine, which grinds and aerates the chocolate to refine the texture and make it extremely smooth. Conching for a long period makes the chocolate flow evenly and enhances its flavor and aroma. Around the same time, he experimented with adding cocoa butter to the chocolate paste before conching, which rendered the chocolate more malleable and less acrid. The result of these two groundbreaking innovations

was fondant chocolate. After twenty years of chocolate production, Lindt decided to sell his company and in 1899 accepted an offer of 1.5 million gold francs made by David Sprüngli, a chocolate manufacturer from Zurich. He could not have foreseen it, but Lindt had just sold the goose that lays the golden eggs.

David Sprüngli's grandfather, Richard Sprüngli, the founder of the family business, came from the same type of modest background as Philippe Suchard, and like him took an early interest in chocolate. After an apprenticeship with a renowned confectioner in Zurich, he bought his own shop in 1845 and embarked on chocolate production. In 1900, he opened a chocolate factory near Zurich. Sprüngli believed that drinking chocolate should be made available to the working classes, in order to improve the deplorable nutritional habits of adults and children alike. Today, after five generations Lindt-Sprüngli is Switzerland's largest independent chocolate manufacturer. It is a veritable institution, an empire which celebrated its 150th anniversary in 1995 by sending a box of chocolates to 2.4 million Swiss families.

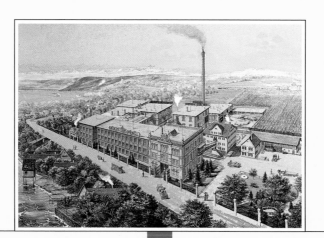

In 1899, Rodolphe Lindt, known during the 1880s as "Monsieur Chocolat," sold his factory in Kilchberg on the lake of Zurich, along with his secret recipe for fondant chocolate, to David Sprüngli for the sum of 1.5 million gold francs (above). Each generation of the Sprüngli dynasty has maintained the firm's independence and progressively modernized the Lindt-Sprüngli factory, which today is highly profitable (facing page, scenes from the early twentieth century). Anybody can purchase one of the three thousand Lindt-Sprüngli shares currently on the market for the price of a gold ingot. The exotic specialty known as "Russian mousse," which capitalized on a brief vogue for Russia early in the century, is no longer available (facing page).

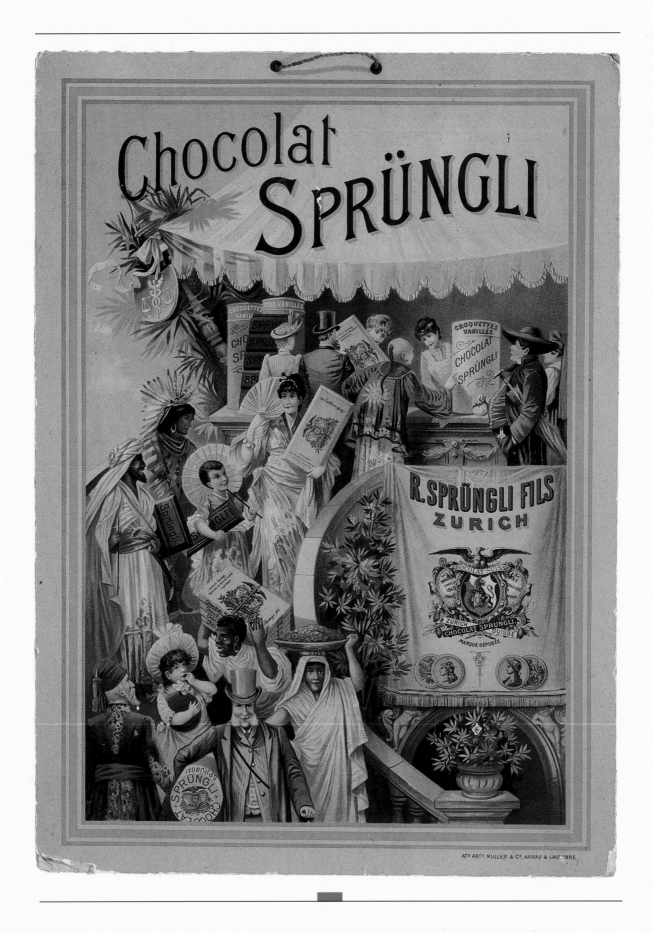

PRALINE AND TOBLERONE

Praline is another tradition that originated in Switzerland, where it made its first appearance at the beginning of the twentieth century. This delicious confection is composed of richly flavored chocolate to which caramelized sugar, well-roasted almonds or hazelnuts, and vanilla have been added. It differs from Italian gianduja, in which the almonds and hazelnuts are only lightly roasted and the sugar is neither caramelized nor melted. The recipe for the Nestlé praline bar, Frigor, was created by Alexandre Cailler in 1923. Savoring a small piece by letting it melt slowly in your mouth is a moment of pure pleasure. The praline bar's closely guarded secret recipe has remained unchanged since 1923, and despite many imitations, has never been equaled.

Munz chocolates, made by a family concern founded in 1874, are another example of the Swiss taste for praline. Munz chocolate sticks, filled with hazelnut cream and rolled in chopped hazelnuts, are only one of the vast array of Swiss pralines. Soon, every manufacturer had its own praline to

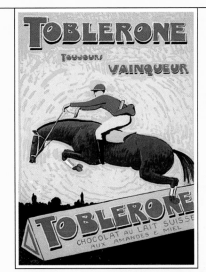

offer: the celebrated Lingots d'Or by Favarger in Geneva; Giandor by Max and Robert Frey; and Torino and Ragusa by Camille Bloch.

The classic Toblerone bar, whose triangular form was designed to recall the Swiss Alps, was created in 1908. Its name was judiciously derived from that of its inventor, Jean Tobler, and the word *torrone*, the Italian nougat made from honey, almond slivers, and egg whites, which is blended with the chocolate. Since 1970, Toblerone bars have been manufactured in Bern by Suchard, which produces 130 tons a day. The smallest Toblerone bar weighs 1.25 ounces and the largest, nearly 10 pounds.

The Swiss, the last to arrive on the chocolate scene, are now the world leaders. Milk chocolate, fondant chocolate, and praline have become such an integral part of the Swiss heritage that the Swiss government advises chocolate manufacturers to keep one year's advance supply of raw materials in stock at all times. These supplies are stored in warehouses hidden away in the Alps. In Switzerland, even chocolate is kept in the bank.

Sprüngli's early twentieth-century advertising campaigns sought to attract an elegant, international clientele. A typical poster features a bevy of cosmopolitan dignitaries arriving to commit the sin of gluttony at R. Sprüngli Fils in Zurich (facing page). One of the posters, perhaps even the first, used by Jean Tobler to launch Toblerone, shows the inimitable triangular bar whose shape evokes the Matterhorn (top). Another advertising image for Sprüngli's drinking chocolate shows a charming serving girl wearing a delicate lace cap over her ringlets and carrying a tray of hot chocolate (above).

ITALIAN CHOCOLATE
Hazelnuts and Gianduja

What is the secret of the gianduja's success? Is it the attractive shape of the small, slightly rounded triangles which are wrapped in festive silver or gold foil? Or is it the luscious, mild, and creamy taste? Indeed, the flavor of the true gianduja is such a subtle blend of hazelnuts and chocolate that it is almost impossible to recognize the individual ingredients by taste alone. Chocolate connoisseurs consider the gianduja to be the highest expression of Italian chocolate and the best example of the now-classic combination of chocolate and hazelnuts, which was first produced in Italy. Today, other nuts, such as walnuts and almonds, sometimes replace the hazelnuts, but the principle of the finely blended gianduja remains the same.

TURIN, THE CHOCOLATE CAPITAL

The gianduja was created in Turin, once the capital of the former duchy of Savoy, in the Piedmont region of Italy, which

borders on France and Switzerland. The cacao bean first arrived in the Piedmont in 1559, when the exiled duke of Savoy, Emmanuel-Philibert, returned to power following the signing of the Treaty of Cateau-Cambrésis by Henri II of France and Philip II of Spain. Emmanuel-Philibert had lived for many years at the court of Philip II's father, Holy Roman Emperor Charles V, and had discovered the delights of chocolate in Spain. The duke's cooks and pastry chefs were familiar with the uses of the beans, and chocolate became known throughout the duchy. Demand rose and, with it, production. By the end of the seventeenth century, 750 pounds of chocolate were being produced daily. Here, as elsewhere, chocolate was first consumed as a beverage and Turin soon became known for a number of specialty drinks. First, the "bavareisa" (Bavarian) was invented, but it was soon surpassed in popularity by the "bicerin," a mixture of coffee and chocolate served in a small glass (a *bicerin* in Italian). Alexandre Dumas was so captivated by this "excellent chocolate drink" when he

The *Gentile delle Langhe*, a particularly flavorful variety of hazelnut that grows in the wild hills south of Turin, became in 1865 the basic ingredient of the now-classic Italian gianduja, a felicitous marriage of flavors today appreciated the world over (above). All chocolate manufacturers in the Po valley make their own type of gianduja, though methods and recipes are veiled in secrecy. The elegant Stratta shop, on the magnificent Piazza San Carlo in Turin, purveyor to the royal house of Savoy and the count of Cavour, is the only Italian confectionery to propose a giant-sized "grangianduja," the downfall of all chocolate lovers. It can be sliced and enjoyed at will (facing page).

passed through Turin in 1852, that he counted its flavor among the most unforgettable experiences of his visit to the beautiful city.

In 1861, the newly unified Italian kingdom was facing serious financial difficulties and the government imposed import quotas on luxury goods, including cacao beans. In response, ingenious Italian chocolate makers formulated a mixture of cocoa powder and finely ground hazelnuts to allow them to use lesser quantities of the expensive commodity. The hazelnut is a traditional Piedmontese product, and the variety the Italians call *Gentile delle Langhe*, which grows in the wild hills south of Turin, is rich in aromatic oil and blends perfectly with chocolate. The most celebrated form of gianduja in Italy was invented by Caffarel, today one of Italy's foremost chocolate manufacturers. In 1865, in honor of the World's Fair, Caffarel introduced small, individually wrapped chocolates filled with this delicious hazelnut and chocolate paste, which it dubbed "gianduiotti."

Today, the Piedmont can boast a great selection of traditional confectioners, all of whom make gianduiotti using their own secret recipes. The celebrated Peyrano firm, located in Turin, makes gianduiotti based on the original recipe, which does not include any milk. Peyrano's gianduiotti and other chocolates are made according to time-honored, artisanal methods and are renowned for their exceptional quality. Peyrano is the only chocolate maker in Turin to make bicerin paste, a mixture of bitter chocolate, honey, cocoa,

and hazelnuts which is sold in pots. Created in honor of one of Turin's earliest chocolate specialties, it is used in place of sugar to sweeten coffee. The Streglio company, founded in 1924, adds milk, sugar, and natural vanilla to the hazelnuts in its gianduiotti and uses three varieties of cacao bean: Carupano, Arriba SSS and Trinidad.

CHOCOLATE IN NORTHERN AND SOUTHERN ITALY

Majani's Fiat Cremino is just as creamy, if not more so, than the gianduja, and certainly is just as sought after by chocolate connoisseurs. Majani, Italy's oldest confectionery, was founded in Bologna in 1796. In 1911, the firm introduced the Fiat Cremino to honor the launching of the Fiat Tipo 4 automobile. The small square of soft fondant chocolate is composed of layers of milk chocolate and hazelnuts alternating with dark chocolate and almonds. Majani's delightful shop on the Via Carbonesi still makes their traditional house specialty, the Gianduja Ingot, which is sold by the slice, but only in winter because of the delicate confection's propensity to melt. Another Majani specialty are "scorze," small sticks of chocolate whose recipe dates from 1832. The scorze have a delicious, bittersweet flavor, the result of a judicious addition of a small quantity of powdered sugar to the chocolate, which is made from four varieties of cacao bean: Seiba Superior, Carupano, and Caracas from Venezuela, and Arriba SSS from Ecuador.

The collection of the Caffarel Museum in Turin contains historic packaging and advertising materials for the brand's first products, including the cinnamon health chocolate, made by Caffarel in the nineteenth century. Gianduiotti were originally made by hand using molds (facing page, bottom). Today, custom-designed machinery developed by Caffarel engineers makes these delicious gianduiotti available to chocolate lovers all over the world (above). In 1911, Senator Agnelli asked the Majani company of Bologna to grant him exclusive rights to their Cremino, composed of four types of chocolate, for the launch of the Fiat Tipo 4 automobile. Ever since, Italians have called this delicacy the "Fiat" Cremino (right).

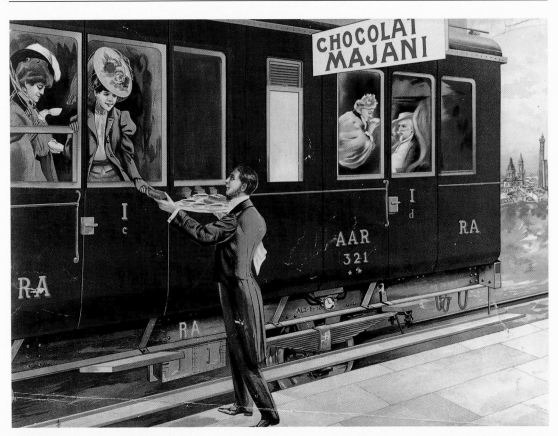

Other quality manufacturers and artisanal chocolate makers have invented lesser-known specialties. The prestigious Romanengo firm, founded in Genoa in 1780, produces succulent cherries, candied orange peel, and mandarin orange slices dipped in fondant chocolate. In Cuneo, about forty miles from Turin, the Cuba firm has been producing its "cuneesi" since 1925. These delicious fondant chocolate shells are filled with a chocolate cream flavored with Jamaican rum. The celebrated café and pastry shop, Rivoire, on the Piazza della Signoria in Florence, enchants customers with its delicious hot chocolate and the old-fashioned chocolate paste sold in elegant red cardboard boxes. Finally, Gay-Odin, founded in Naples in 1893, offers its original "bombonati" garnished with a roasted cacao bean to bring out the authentic flavor of chocolate.

LOVE AND CHOCOLATE

The most popular chocolates in Italy are unquestionably the hazelnut- or cherry- filled varieties, which are sold at café bars to be enjoyed with espresso. Particularly popular are Perugina's Baci, creamy chocolates filled with cocoa paste and chopped, roasted hazelnuts. The word *baci* means kisses in Italian, and lovers have been exchanging the chocolates since 1922 to discover the trademark romantic messages concealed under the elegant silver wrapper. Today, Baci are exported all over the world at the rate of half a billion a day. Baci are in direct competition with Ferrero's Rochers, which are roasted-hazelnut-paste centers coated with fondant chocolate. Rochers are the best-selling Italian chocolate worldwide, while Mon Chéri, the leading cherry liqueur chocolate, is enormously successful in both Italy and Germany.

A nation of artists, the Italians will never cease to amaze and delight with their imaginative creations. An example of Italian inventiveness is the chocolate spread Nutella, launched in 1949, when chocolate prices were still extremely inflated following the Second World War. Nutella is made of a vegetable paste consisting of hazelnuts, sugar, and skimmed milk, and contains only a small proportion of low-fat cocoa. For postwar Europe, Nutella fulfilled the dream of an affordable delicacy, available to everyone. A generation of Europeans grew up on Nutella, and today many adults are still quite fond of it; one Parisian publisher we spoke with admitted to eating it by the spoonful. For modern French children, Nutella is still a favorite at breakfast or for after-school snacks. Neither its formula, nor the glass jar in which it is sold (a modern version of the *bicerin*) have changed since 1949. And yet, despite the success of Nutella and other Italian specialties, Italy for chocolate connoisseurs is above all the country of the gianduja.

Giuseppe Majani, a highly creative chocolate maker from Bologna, had one ambition: to sell his products to the most elegant society in Italy and Europe. The resulting Majani publicity campaigns were somewhat naïve, but set an example for other firms. Slogans included "The indispensable Majani stop on the Trans-Europe-Express" (facing page, top), and "The Majani chocolate break during the cabinet meeting," in which the ministers of the day were pictured (bottom). In 1922, Giovanni Buitoni invented the Bacio, the popular Italian chocolate "kiss," which has delighted generations of lovers. The elegant Baci package was designed by the celebrated artist Federico Seneca (above).

BELGIAN CHOCOLATE
The Kingdom of Pralines

Léonidas, Godiva, and Neuhaus are names which have made Belgian chocolate famous. Chocolate manufactured in Belgium has an easily recognizable taste and is much appreciated by lovers of soft textures and rich flavors. In France and the United States, a liking for Belgian chocolate has become a national infatuation, and many French chocolate makers, like Jeff de Bruges and De Neuville, have been greatly influenced by their northern neighbors.

The unique flavor of Belgian chocolate as we know it today could not have existed without the ingenuity of Jean Neuhaus—also the inventor of the "ballotin"—who in 1912 developed the first hard chocolate shell. Previously, fillings had to have a relatively firm consistency to allow handling and chocolate coating. The arrival of the Neuhaus shell marked the end of these restrictions, because these small, solid recipients could contain almost fluid creams, soft caramels, light ganache, or pralines too unctuous to be worked independently. The Belgians have been so successful with this creamy whipped filling that the term "praline" has become almost synonymous with Belgian chocolate.

Pralines may differ in composition depending on the manufacturer, but not in richness, flavor, texture, or in their generous dimen-sions. It takes two or three bites of a Manon to appreciate all of its subtlety. This praline is certainly the best-known example of the Belgian chocolate-maker's art, although in fact the original Manon recipe does not contain a single ounce of chocolate. It can only be made by hand and is composed of a coffee-flavored buttercream pressed between two walnut halves and dipped in a hot sugar fondant. Although Corné-Dynastie, Godiva of Brussels, and De Hucorne-Fronville of Namur still make traditional Manons, practically all other firms have replaced the sugar with white chocolate, which is mild and sweet and contains no cocoa solids. These very creamy pralines, coated with white, dark, or milk chocolate, and with a high cocoa butter content, have a truly unique taste because of a skillful contrast of textures and flavors; they are at once soft and brittle, creamy and crunchy, sweet and bitter. Still, the *crème de la crème* of Belgian chocolate are fresh cream pralines, which, in fact, have a buttercream center which has been beaten and emulsified until it becomes too light to handle, and is flavored with Cointreau, coffee, chocolate, pineapple, vanilla, or raspberry. Because they are fragile and do not keep well, they should be consumed quickly. When the smooth, shiny chocolate shell breaks open, the

Although Godiva chocolates are sold in over forty countries, traditional manufacturing methods have been preserved, including the grinding of cacao beans (facing page). Godiva rigidly adheres to the production and quality-control procedures required by law to obtain the "chocolat belge" appellation, and at the same time continuing European gourmet traditions. It is hardly surprising that Godiva chocolates enjoy such great international success, particularly in the United States.

voluptuous texture and flavor of the "fresh cream" can be appreciated to the fullest.

Although Belgium is above all famous for pralines, other types of traditional Belgian chocolate also enjoy a solid reputation. Chocolate production in Belgium began in the nineteenth century, when vessels loaded with sacks of cacao beans arrived at the port of Antwerp. In 1870, Charles Neuhaus, father of the inventor of pralines, was the first to open a small chocolate firm, which he named Côte d'Or. The company participated in successive World's Fairs where Europeans had the opportunity to discover the intense flavor of these generous bars of dark chocolate. In 1906, a trumpeting elephant was selected as the firm's trademark, to symbolize the strength of Côte d'Or chocolate. Today this tradition continues and a redesigned pachyderm still graces the red wrappers of the many varieties of Côte d'Or chocolate bars.

Charles Callebaut began producing chocolate later than his compatriots, but his solid chocolate and cream-filled bars, sold under the name of Meurisse, continue to be greatly appreciated, while professional and home cooks from Liège to Bruges still break off pieces of Callebaut's famous 1 pound bar of baking chocolate to make mousses or cakes for a traditional Sunday lunch. After the Second World War, Charles Callebaut came up with the ingenious idea of supplying manufacturers with chocolate not in its usual dried "cake"

form, but as a hot liquid transported in tanker trucks. This practical, cost-saving system has since become widespread. The firm still supplies its virtually "made-to-order" couverture chocolates and other products to artisanal and industrial manufacturers in Belgium, France, England, and the United States. Other historic Belgian firms which are still thriving today include Jacques, founded in 1896, which in 1936 used the basic praline concept to create cream-filled bars, twenty-three varieties of which are still manufactured today; the Jean Galler company, which also produces bars and a chocolate spread; and Bruyerre, founded in 1909 near Brussels and very much appreciated for its refined, cognac-flavored caramel ganache and rum-flavored dark ganache.

In addition to these traditional manufacturers, the best-known name in Belgian chocolate is probably Henri Wittamer, and gourmets have been flocking to the Wittamer store on the Place du Grand Sablon in Brussels since 1910. Every chocolate lover knows Wittamer's famous cake, which is composed of two contrasting chocolate mousses, one light and the other dark, and his chestnut and chocolate "délice," both of which melt in the mouth as they release their fine flavors. Wittamer also sells sixty-eight varieties of pralines, including fifteen made with fresh cream. With its heavenly pralines and traditional chocolates, Belgium has paid a fitting tribute to cacao, "food of the gods."

This advertisement for Jacques, a chocolate manufacturer based in Verviers, shows the celebrated praline bars introduced in 1936 (facing page, top). Before specializing, starting in 1925, almost exclusively in the production of fine couverture chocolates, the Callebaut firm produced chocolate candy, like the Salvator bar, launched in 1911 (facing page). The origins of Léonidas date back to 1910, when Léonidas Kesdekidis, a Greek American, came to Belgium for the World's Fair. Founded in 1911, Léonidas today has over 1,650 stores throughout the world (facing page). Also in 1910, Alphonse Delhaize, a grocer in Brussels, began to sell his own brand of chocolate (above).

DUTCH
CHOCOLATE
Fragrant Hot Chocolate

The creamy, frothy cup of steaming hot chocolate we enjoy on a cold winter's day is a pleasure we owe in great part to the Dutch. During the seventeenth century, vessels flying the Dutch flag crossed the seas transporting sugar, tobacco, and cacao beans, and unloaded their precious cargoes in Amsterdam. However, it was not until two centuries later that the power of the windmills on the banks of the nearby river Zaan was used to grind cacao beans. At the first Dutch chocolate manufacturing sites, founded at the end of the seventeenth century, horses or oxen turned the grindstones. Production was very limited, and until the end of the eighteenth century, elegant porcelain cups filled with hot chocolate were only to be seen in the homes of wealthy Dutch financiers. In those days the subtle beverage was prepared by first grating and then dissolving a small tablet of chocolate paste in hot milk or water. The paste, which solidified on cooling, was obtained by heating ground cacao beans with vanilla, cinnamon, and sometimes even ambergris.

Honey or cane sugar were added to the chocolate pot to temper the bitter taste. Gradually, the custom of offering guests a cup of hot chocolate became generalized among elegant society.

COCOA POWDER

A revolutionary development in Dutch chocolate production occured in 1778, when the owners of a windmill near Amsterdam stopped grinding mustard seeds and started to process cacao beans instead. Twenty-five years later, approximately thirty chocolate manufacturers were operating a battery of windmills. In 1815, a certain Coenraad Van Houten took over one of these chocolate factories in Amsterdam. For many years, makers of drinking chocolate had been trying unsuccessfully to separate out the various components of chocolate paste, in particular the fatty substance known as cocoa butter which tended to separate and rise to the top. The breakthrough came in 1825, when Van Houten invented a

At the beginning of the eighteenth century, Dutch vessels began to transport colonial products from the Americas, and the port of Amsterdam soon became the major clearing house for cacao bean imports. However, only 50 percent of the beans remained in the country, where they were ground in windmills to make the celebrated Dutch cocoa powder (above: a windmill in Zaandam). According to the Guiness Book of World Records, Mrs. Jenny van Aken has a collection of over 2,800 antique chocolate tins, which are charming reminders of the history of Dutch chocolate (facing page). Following double page: a venerable windmill where cacao seeds are ground, though the mill was originally designed to grind mustard seeds.

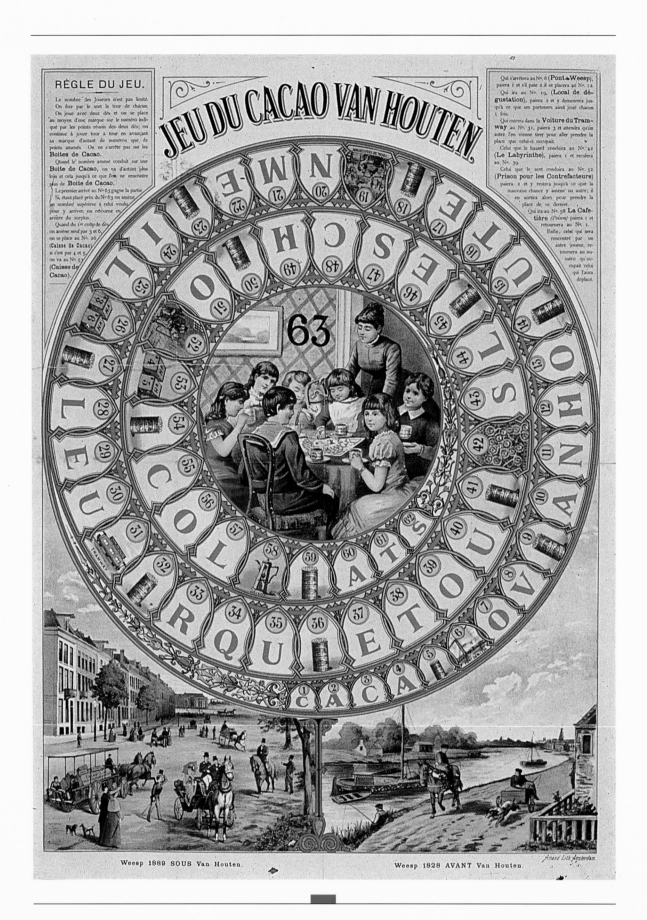

hydraulic press—known as a cocoa press—which extracted the cocoa butter, leaving behind a dry, powdery residue. This "cake," as it is termed, was easy to pulverize, producing a fine, light powder which dissolved readily in hot milk. This was a vast improvement over the thick paste then in use, which was greasy and difficult to melt. Van Houten patented his invention in 1828 and it was soon adopted by chocolate manufacturers throughout Europe. He also developed another process, known as "dutching," which involved the addition of potash to improve the solubility of the powder. Instant chocolate drinks had come into being, and yellow packets of Van Houten's Unsweetened Cocoa were soon to be found in kitchens everywhere. All cocoa powder needed was a little sugar, banana flour, or malt extract to obtain delicious, nourishing beverage mixes like Banania, a European favorite, or the classic Ovaltine.

The repercussions of Van Houten's discovery went beyond the realm of drinking chocolate. Chocolate manufacturers now had at their disposal a new and intriguing substance known as cocoa butter. This "butter"—the basic ingredient of white chocolate—melts at human body temperature and, when mixed with chocolate before the conching phase, adds remarkable creaminess and malleability. The addition of cocoa butter rendered chocolate supple enough to be molded into bars, figurines, or drops, a tradition at the Dutch firm Droste, or

L'ALIMENT PRESCRIT PAR LE MEDECIN.
Une chambre à coucher à Hindelooper (Hollande).
T.s.v.p.

even formed to represent letters of the alphabet. When Bensdorp founded his chocolate plant in Amsterdam, this discovery enabled him to manufacture individually wrapped bars rather than weighing out loose chocolate.

At the time of Van Houten's inventions, the Netherlands imported a large percentage of the world cacao-bean crop. However, Dutch firms gradually began to specialize in the production of cocoa powder rather than in the manufacture of eating chocolate. The four great names which dominated the nineteenth century in Holland, Van Houten, Bensdorp, De Zaan, and Gerkens, still exist today. They supply the world with high-quality, slightly bitter cocoa powder, in which the French roll their truffles, which the Italians sprinkle on their tiramisu and cappuccino, and which the Austrians use to make their celebrated Viennese hot chocolate.

The Netherlands is essentially an egalitarian country, and nowhere is this more amply demonstated than in the traditional ceremony that takes place every year at the royal palace on Christmas Day, which also happens to be the queen's birthday. Her Majesty is the perfect hostess as she stands behind a table laden with brioches, pastries, and other delicacies, personally serving hot chocolate to her staff and the members of the court who are invited for the occasion. For the Dutch, this delicious beverage is as much a part of their daily lives as the cultivation of tulips.

In 1895 the "Cacao Van Houten" game was devised by an anonymous Frenchman. Inspired by a popular game similar to snakes and ladders, it was a clever marketing ploy to attract children, who would ask their parents to buy only Van Houten cocoa (facing page). Gérard Droste hired the celebrated poster designer Cassandre (1901–1968) to create a memorable logo to symbolize the brand and imprint it on the minds of consumers. The result was the introduction of the "Droste man," which considerably boosted sales of all Droste products (left). Advertisements for Van Houten often emphasized the medicinal and therapeutic powers of chocolate (above).

AUSTRIAN AND GERMAN CHOCOLATE
The Art of Pastry

The pithy phrase, "the fine arts are five in number: painting, sculpture, music, poetry, and architecture, whose principal branch is pastry-making" is attributed to Marie-Antoine Carême, a French chef who traveled to Austria in the entourage of Talleyrand and who remained in the country as a chef at the imperial court.

It is true that Austrians and German pastry-chefs excel in their art. Their most legendary creations are, respectively, the celebrated Viennese Sacher torte and the rich German Black Forest cake, a velvety combination of chocolate, sugar, and whipped cream garnished with Morello cherries and kirsch. The tradition of hot chocolate, which in German is called *Trinkschokolade* or *heisse Schokolade*, is kept alive by the respect for their history which characterizes both countries. A recipe for hot chocolate by the cup was developed at the beginning of the eighteenth century. During the same period, the celebrated porcelain factories of Vienna, Nymphenburg, Meissen, Berlin, and Brunswick began to produce elegant hot chocolate services to honor the exquisite beverage. At the time, it was strongly recommended by some connoisseurs to dissolve the cocoa in Spanish or German wine and to season it with pepper.

Ravaged by the Thirty Years' War (1618–1648), Germany remained relatively indifferent to the exotic vogues which had caught on in other European countries. For decades, chocolate in Germany was used only for medicinal purposes and was sold exclusively by apothecaries. The Dutch doctor Cornelius Bontekoe was instrumental in promoting the consumption of chocolate, because of his influential position as personal physician to the Great Elector, Frederick William of Brandenburg (1620–1688). One of the Great Elector's most celebrated successors, King Frederick II of Prussia, (1712–1786), known to history as Frederick the Great, levied a tax on this exotic luxury to control imports. Not wanting to be deprived of his favorite beverage, the enlightened monarch

Delicious, typically Viennese hot chocolate is served with a topping of fresh whipped cream at the Schwarzenberg Palace café, now a luxury hotel (top). Once the official suppliers to the imperial court and holders of the prestigious appellation of *königlich und kaiserlich* (royal and imperial), Demel today is a living monument to the refined pleasures of chocolate confectionery and pastry (left).

asked the scientist Andreas Sigismund Margraff, inventor of a process for extracting sugar from beets to replace expensive cane sugar, to find a less costly substitute for chocolate using the blossoms and seeds of the lime tree!

German reactions to chocolate differed from city to city. In Berlin, it was considered to be an unpleasant, but fortifying tonic. However, the "drink of the gods" was a triumph in Dresden, which boasted one of the most brilliant and elegant courts in Europe. The same was true in Leipzig, where the fashionable Felsche café expanded to conform to the vogue

for *Schokoladestuben*, which allowed polite society to meet over a cup of chocolate. During the nineteenth century, chocolate was to provide a source of inspiration for Goethe, who corresponded regularly with the Leipzig-based chocolate maker Riquet.

The great German hot-chocolate tradition has not disappeared and is particularly well honored at the Café König in Baden-Baden, where the beverage is still prepared with fondant chocolate (preferably Belgian or French), fresh milk, natural vanilla beans, cane sugar, a pinch of cinnamon, and a dash of salt and pepper.

The Imperial torte, a square chocolate cake with five thin layers of almond paste, was created by a master pastry chef at the court of Emperor Franz Joseph (1830–1916). Along with the fabulous Sacher torte, named after Metternich's inspired chef who created the recipe in 1832, it is one of the great masterpieces of Viennese pastry. Individual orders received by the Hotel Sacher, the Hotel Imperial, and Demel are dispatched to the four corners of the earth in magnificent wooden boxes (above).

Contemporary German chocolate manufacturers also maintain the same traditional standards. Since 1865 Rebel has regaled the small hot-spring resort town of Bad Reichenhall with its selection of fine chocolates, while in Berlin, Rausch attracts an elegant clientele with its pralines and extra thin chocolate bars made from Java cacao beans. The chocolate sold by Hachez, based in Bremen since 1890, is

made exclusively with cacao beans from the high plateaus of Venezuela and Ecuador, and is flavored with the finest Bourbon or Madagascar vanilla. Acclaimed by chocolate connoisseurs all over the world, Coppeneur truffles, with triple fillings and liquid centers, are made exclusively in the town of Siegburg in Westphalia. The chocolates made by the renowned Asbach distillery, located in Rüdesheim am Rhein, were originally developed to resolve a delicate problem of etiquette. During the 1920s, it was considered unseemly for a lady to drink alcohol in public. The firm decided to circumvent this prohibition by creating its now-famous brandy chocolates, in which a thin layer of sugar separates the liqueur from the chocolate. Founded in 1860, Imhoff-Stollwerk is the largest chocolate manufacturer in Germany. The impressive modern headquarters on the banks of the Elbe river is a fitting symbol of the corporation's chocolate empire. The Imhoff-Stollwerk Chocolate Museum boasts a tropical greenhouse planted with cacao saplings and a gallery displaying an array of automatic vending machines, the most elaborate of which resemble old-fashioned grandfather clocks.

Goethe (1749–1832) was thirty-eight years old when J.H.W. Tischbein painted a portrait of the writer set in a Roman landscape (top, detail). During his travels, Goethe frequently wrote to his wife asking her to send his favorite chocolate from Riquet. Goethe also corresponded for many years with Jean George Riquet, the founder of this establishment, on the beneficial effects of chocolate on the health. In 1794, Goethe struck up a friendship with the poet Schiller (1759–1805), who, like him, was extremely fond of hot chocolate (above).

ROYAL AND IMPERIAL PASTRIES

The art of pastry-making was held in high esteem at the Austrian imperial court, where the master pastry chef was decorated with almost as many medals as a victorious general. Chocolate as a beverage was known in Austria as early as the sixteenth century, but it made a fairly late entry into pastry-making; the first known recipe for a chocolate cake dates only to 1778. However, true inspiration was lacking until Metternich's head chef, Franz Sacher, had a flash of inspiration one night in 1832, which led to the creation of the most famous chocolate cake in the world, the Sacher torte. This sublime pastry is a subtle blend of chocolate, eggs, and butter, with a thin layer of apricot glaze in the middle and a dark, glossy chocolate frosting. The success of the Sacher torte triggered a war between the Hotel Sacher and Demel, the incomparable "k.u.k." pastry-maker (*königlich und kaiserlich*, or royal and imperial).

Today, Demel is a living symbol of the Viennese pastry tradition. The firm even has its own version of the Sacher torte, based on a recipe which Franz Sacher's son Edward gave to

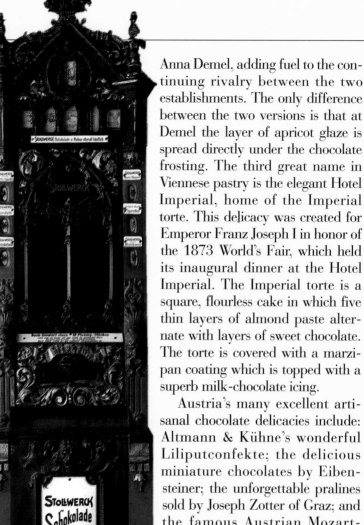

Anna Demel, adding fuel to the continuing rivalry between the two establishments. The only difference between the two versions is that at Demel the layer of apricot glaze is spread directly under the chocolate frosting. The third great name in Viennese pastry is the elegant Hotel Imperial, home of the Imperial torte. This delicacy was created for Emperor Franz Joseph I in honor of the 1873 World's Fair, which held its inaugural dinner at the Hotel Imperial. The Imperial torte is a square, flourless cake in which five thin layers of almond paste alternate with layers of sweet chocolate. The torte is covered with a marzipan coating which is topped with a superb milk-chocolate icing.

Austria's many excellent artisanal chocolate delicacies include: Altmann & Kühne's wonderful Liliputconfekte; the delicious miniature chocolates by Eibensteiner; the unforgettable pralines sold by Joseph Zotter of Graz; and the famous Austrian Mozartkugeln, or Mozart cake, made of luscious pistachio marzipan balls covered with nougat and frosted with a chocolate glaze. Although originally created in Salzburg, the best Mozartkugeln can be savored at Schun in Badgastein. Austrian pastries and chocolates are well worth the journey, wherever the search for them may lead.

During the 1870s, Heinrich Imhoff and Ludwig Stollwerk applied a strategy of technical innovation, industrial investment, and dynamic marketing to mold the modest company they had inherited into the leading chocolate manufacturer in the world. The Gothic "cathedral," (above) made of painted metal, is, in reality, an example of the automatic chocolate vending machines which were once in widespread use throughout Germany. Superb examples of these beautiful machines can be seen in the Imhoff-Stollwerk Chocolate Museum in Cologne.

CHOCOLATE IN GREAT BRITAIN AND THE UNITED STATES

From Cadbury and Hershey to Handmade Chocolate

In Great Britain and the United States, the national taste for chocolate was developed principally by great industrial firms. Nevertheless, interest in fine, artisanal chocolate is growing, and on both sides of the Atlantic homegrown talent is challenging the best that continental Europe has to offer.

Few countries have as strong a preference for sweet foods as England. This is, in part, a result of the opening of sugar-producing mills in the British West Indies during the eighteenth and nineteenth centuries, which rendered sugar a food that the middle and lower classes could afford. Indeed, they made it a staple of their diet, drinking heavily sweetened tea—a product promoted by another government-owned monopoly, the British East India Company.

British industry and commerce were developing rapidly and the confectionery sector was no exception. In 1824, John Cadbury opened a store in Birmingham, where he sold tea, coffee, and chocolate. A fervent Quaker, he believed that chocolate was a nourishing, healthy drink (at the time, it was consumed principally as a beverage), and should be sold as a replacement for gin in the daily diets of the working classes. Using Van Houten's cocoa press and dutching process to make their hot cocoa powder, the Cadburys and their fellow Quaker chocolate manufacturers—the Frys, the Rowntrees, and the Terrys—were instrumental in making chocolate, hitherto a luxury item, available on a wide scale. George and Richard Cadbury, who shared the ardent Quaker convictions of their father John, established the model village of Bournville in 1879, where workers were provided with free education, healthcare, and community services. By 1894, Cadbury had become the largest chocolate manufacturer in Great Britain and today its confections are known throughout the world.

British industrial chocolate has an extremely high sugar content, as befits national taste, while the content of cocoa solids is relatively low. Great Britain also seems to prefer milk chocolate to any other kind: milk chocolate bars made by Cadbury, Mars, and Rowntree are immensely popular.

Another national favorite is mint chocolate—a quintessentially British combination of dark chocolate filled with peppermint fondant. The best-known makers of these are Bendicks, whose Bittermints are still a classic after-dinner

In 1900, Queen Victoria sent her New Year's greetings to the British troops stationed in South Africa during the Boer War in the form of a specially molded chocolate bar (above). English firms have always been particularly innovative in the development of new products. Ever since the early days of the chocolate trade, consumers have been able to choose from among a wide variety of chocolate bars, tins of assorted chocolates, candies, or creams (facing page).

offering, and Rowntree, with its After Eights. Smaller-scale firms have been fulfilling the demand for good chocolate since the nineteenth century, but their number has increased significantly in recent years. The historic leaders are Charbonnel et Walker and Prestat, two hallowed central London chocolate shops. Of the two, connoisseurs currently favor Charbonnel et Walker, which is located in the Royal Arcade on Old Bond Street, near the site of the original store founded in 1875. While still Prince of Wales, Edward VII (1841–1910) invited the French chocolate maker, Madame Charbonnel, to leave the Maison Boissier in Paris to establish a fine confectionery shop in London with an English colleague, Mrs. Walker.

The royal cachet and the quality products helped to build the lasting loyalty of the carriage trade, which continues to this day; despite having changed hands several times (the firm returned to private ownership in 1989), the shop still proudly displays the royal warrant.

The two most highly regarded private chocolate makers in London, Gerard Ronay and Sara Jayne, work in the French and Belgian traditions, but have adapted continental methods to British tastes. Trained in France, Gerard Ronay's most unusual and successful truffles include smoked lemon, geranium, dill, and rose, as well as gooseberry and rhubarb, the stars of English crumbles and puddings. Another product that appeals to

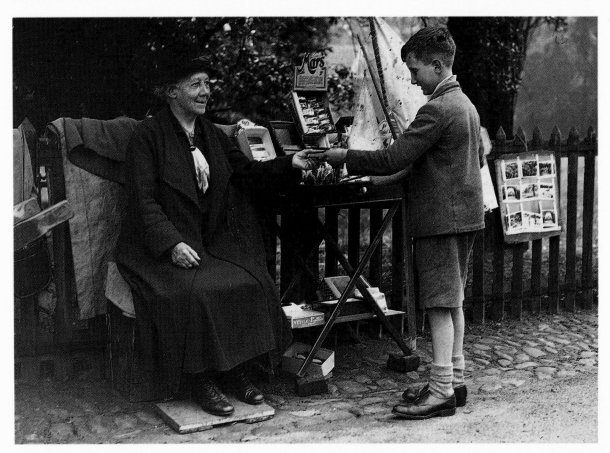

British taste are his thin, rectangular after-dinner mints. In Ronay's chocolate, restraint is married to deep flavor, although nothing overwhelms. In contrast, Sara Jayne takes a more robust approach with her lush, Belgian-style handmade truffles, which combine the melting texture of fillings made with fresh Devon cream and an enrobing of hard, crunchy milk- or dark-chocolate, with a final dusting of cocoa powder.

The pulsing heart of the British chocolate-loving world is a tiny Chelsea shop called Rococo.

Here Chantal Coady, the French-born owner and author of several books on chocolate, imports French and Belgian chocolates extremely high in cocoa solids, and searches out the best small makers of English chocolate. The flavorings of her distinctive handmade chocolate bars include Earl Grey tea, juniper, thyme, lavender, cardamom, orange-flower water, pink peppercorn, toasted coconut, caramelized almonds, and crystallized ginger. Thanks to the skill of these and other fine artisans, British chocolate can be counted among the finest in the world.

The legendary Mrs. Wheelabread of Kensington Gardens, who was known as the "chocolate lady," sold small toys and candies to children before the Second World War, including the famous Mars Bar (above). This classic advertising image for Cadbury shows the bus to Bournville, the model village founded in 1879 by George and Richard Cadbury for Cadbury employees. Roald Dahl's celebrated children's book, *Charlie and the Chocolate Factory*, was partially inspired by the village and factory at Bournville.

CHOCOLATE MADE IN THE USA

For Europeans of a certain generation, mass-produced American milk chocolate bars are a symbol of the generosity of the U.S. army troops who distributed government-issued candy to the cheering crowds as they entered newly liberated villages at the end of the Second World War. Chocolate probably arrived in North America via Europe in the mid-eighteenth century. In 1765, Dr. James Baker and his associate John Hannon built a chocolate factory on the banks of the Neponset river in Massachusetts; renamed the Walter Baker Company by John's grandson in 1780, the firm is still in business today. The story of modern American chocolate truly began over a century later, however, with Milton S. Hershey, a caramel manufacturer from Pennsylvania. Hershey, as a young and ambitious man, first saw German chocolate production machinery at the 1893 Chicago World's Fair, and decided that chocolate was the wave of the future. The first Hershey's milk chocolate bar was sold in

For American GIs, a big bar of Whitman's chocolate was one of the best presents patriotic civilians could send, at least according to this advertisement, which appeared in *Life* magazine on 8 February 1943. The end of the Second World War marked a new era in chocolate advertising and image-making, which henceforth would be based on photography rather than the graphic arts.

1895 and the world responded to his ambition. Hershey followed the example of the Cadburys in England and Menier in France, building a model village for his workers and establishing a school for orphaned boys. Today, a best-seller is the venerable Hershey Kiss, introduced by Milton Hershey, in 1907 and currently produced at a rate of close to 30 million per day.

In the United States, the popularity of hand-made, European-style chocolate has bounded forward over the past fifteen years. At the fore-front is Fran Bigelow, who, in 1982, founded Fran's in Seattle. Today, she is the country's best all-around chocolate maker, and the taste of her creations is invariably pleasing without being overwhelming. In addition to classic truf-fles and pralines, Fran's makes the enormously popular Gold Bar—the confection that built the firm's reputation across the country. This sophisticated version of the candy bar, enrobed in mild, dark Belgian Callebaut chocolate, is soft and chewy like Snickers and other mass-produced bars, but infinitely superior in flavor.

Richard H. Donnelly dis-covered extremely young that American chocolates did not meet his standards. After studying chocolate making with the celebrated Robert Linxe in Paris and a stint with the legendary Wittamer firm in Brussels, Donnelly returned to the United States to work for the French choco-latier Jean-Yves Duperret in San Francisco. In 1988, at the age of twenty-three, Donnelly

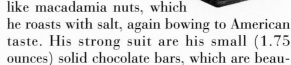

opened a chocolate-pro-duction facility in Santa Cruz, California. All of Donnelly's base choco-lates are made by the French firm Valrhona, but to this European foundation he adds a large dose of American style and ingredients, like macadamia nuts, which he roasts with salt, again bowing to American taste. His strong suit are his small (1.75 ounces) solid chocolate bars, which are beau-tifully packaged and come in several distinc-tive, rich flavors.

Founded in 1988 by Ben Strohecker in Salem, Massachusetts, Harbor Sweets has had enormous success reinventing American favorites. His "flagship" product, called Sweet Sloops, brings extremely high quality to the American love of nuts, chocolate, and caramel. Strohecker offers his employees flexible hours, for example, to accomodate mothers without access to childcare or retired people in need of extra money and companionship. Following in his modest way in the phil-anthropic footsteps of the great chocolate industrialists like Émile Menier, the Cadburys, and Milton Hershey, Ben Stro-hecker, and his enlightened company Harbor Sweets, fit-tingly conclude this survey of the world's greatest names in chocolate.

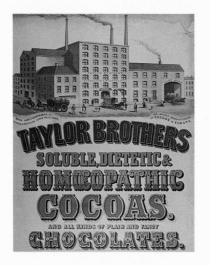

An antique tin for the now-defunct American brand, Huyler's Cocoa. The label specifying the origin of the cocoa—Caracas—was a mark of quality (top). An advertisement for the Taylor Brothers firm, which, in emulation of European apothecaries, entered the homeopathic med-icine market by extolling the curative virtues of chocolate (above). Of the many exotic prod-ucts which the Europeans discovered in the Americas, the cacao bean was among the most valuable. Centuries later, numerous European immigrants to the United States became wholesalers of raw materials, like the young New York cacao bean merchant featured in this photograph from the 1920s (facing page).

THE TASTE
· OF ·
CHOCOLATE

Like the flavor of the scented madeleine dipped in a cup of tea, which launched Marcel Proust on a remarkable journey into his past, the taste of chocolate is one that is intensely redolent of childhood memories. All that is required is a small piece of the right kind of chocolate, which can be dark, white, milk, or filled with cream, fruit, or nuts. The result is instantaneous, although it differs, of course, depending on age, experience, and even nationality. Just close your eyes, and place the chocolate into your mouth, either prolonging the pleasure by letting it melt on your tongue, or eating it quickly, without any preliminaries. As the chocolate softens, the comforting, unmistakable taste transports you into a delightful world of memories. If you are American, the scene may be a traditional after-school snack of milk and chocolate-chip cookies, or a handful of silver-wrapped Hershey's Kisses. If you are French, it might be a thick slice of well-buttered country bread with a crisp, golden-brown crust, smelling deliciously of yeast, and spread with a generous layer of dark chocolate grated with a knife. If you are British, it could be biting into a seemingly enormous Cadbury Easter egg and savoring the deliciously creamy chocolate filling. The memories are often precise and very real, but sometimes they recall habitual activities rather than specific scenes, for example, the thickness of your favorite

cream-filled chocolate cookie, the number you were allowed to have at one time, and the different ways you found to eat them: whole as a sandwich, or carefully separating the two halves to eat the creamy filling first. Sometimes the experience is no more than a fleeting image: an old-fashioned chocolate tin, a kindly grandmother, or the fragrant steam rising from a cup of hot chocolate.

Some people suddenly see themselves on a summer's day battling with a small bar of soft, half-melted milk chocolate, carefully extracting it from its paper wrapper and trying to get it into their mouths rather than all over their hands and faces. Others remember going to pick out a special birthday treat at the local bakery and the delicious smell of freshly baked bread and cakes and the smiling faces of the baker and his wife.

The miraculous powers of chocolate are not limited to allowing us to travel in time, they also let us voyage to other lands. The unforgettable taste of a churro, dipped in hot chocolate as dark and thick as paint can instantly transport us to Spain. The moist, rich flavor of a dense Black Forest cake can take us to a Viennese café, where the strains of a Strauss waltz mingle with the cheerful clatter of dishes and the gentle hum of conversation. A square of sophisticated dark chocolate can take us back to Italy and the delicious chocolate known as "neapolitan" served with the best cappucino in the

Like treasured family heirlooms, chocolate cake recipes are passed down from generation to generation. The dense reine-de-Saba cake pictured on page 162 is certain to delight friends and loved ones. Brillat-Savarin (1755–1826), the celebrated French gastronome, prescribed chocolate as a cure for "ennui." If liqueur chocolates had existed during his lifetime, he certainly would have recognized their fortifying powers (page 163). By 1890, the date of this poster, brands like Poulain, Suchard, Cadbury, and Van Houten were already household names (facing page). Children of all ages look forward to eating traditional chocolate Easter eggs (above).

world. One sip of hot cocoa and we find ourselves in a tea room in London, being served from an elegant porcelain chocolate service, though the taste, texture, and even the temperature of the beverage are far more vivid than the name or location of the establishment.

Memories of chocolate are sometimes selective and even capricious. Although they are almost invariably happy ones, they can often evoke an almost melancholy nostalgia for the past. Assorted chocolate bonbons, for example, can be reminders of family Christmases, when the elaborately decorated boxes always looked enormous and the picture on the lid seemed like a work of art. Inside were pralines, nougats, marzipans, liqueur cherries, and creams, and nobody could decide whether to choose the square ones or the round ones, or the ones wrapped in silver or gold foil. The chocolates, symmetrically arranged in neat rows, diminished in asymmetrical chaos. Certain sensitive souls are overwhelmed by the memory of these moments spent with cherished ones, some of whom are no longer with us, and have difficulty in controlling their emotions. Memories linked with boxes of assorted chocolates need to be handled with caution.

An entire book could be devoted to describing all the emotions chocolate can arouse. One chapter could explore the interesting subject of chocolate cakes, analyzing the phenomenon that cakes made by mothers, which, though perhaps not quite as special as cakes made by grandmothers, were always vastly superior to those made by sisters. This chapter could also discuss shape, icing, and serving temperature, not to mention the incomparable pleasure of scraping the unbaked batter from the bottom of the mixing bowl and licking the spoon. There would also be chapters on chocolate

In this still from the 1927 film *Du sollst nich stehlen*, twenty-two-year-old Lilian Harvey, the darling of the German public, is occupied in the classic modern pursuit of reading novels while eating chocolate bonbons (above). Chocolate was a luxury product until the Second World War and this 1936 photograph shows the fancifully decorated boxes of assorted chocolates which were then a much-coveted item. Even today these lavish boxes immediately evoke festivity, abundance, and variety. Sales are mainly limited to Christmas and Valentine's Day, although chocolate manufacturers would like to see us continue buying all year round.

cupcakes, hot fudge sundaes, and chocolate éclairs. The chapter on chocolate mousse would debate the merits of the large, collective serving bowl versus small, individual ones, or the advantage of adding candied orange peel, candied ginger, glazed chestnuts, or flavored liqueurs to the mousse. The important subject of the delicate wafer which accompanies the mousse would also be discussed, comparing the positions of those who recommend classic ladyfingers and those who lean toward delicate crêpes dentelles, whose paper-thin layers crumble and blend with the mousse. This would conveniently lead to a chapter on cookies and the attributes of the chocolate-filled, the partially or entirely chocolate-coated, or the chocolate-chip.

A sub-section, not entirely devoid of interest, could be devoted to the debate between those who dunk cookies in milk and those who uphold the more traditional munching method when it comes to hob-nobs, chocolate chip cookies, or brownies. The chapter on chocolate confectionery would reveal guilty secrets, such as our continuing affection for the mass-produced candy bars of our childhood, whose milk chocolate coating, although of very inferior quality, still inspires blissful smiles.

The final section would be devoted to adult passions. The sudden, unrestrained urges that can come over the best of us for pure, unadulterated dark or milk chocolate would be explored, along with our sense of well-being

Whether fresh, candied, or dipped, oranges in all their guises are delicious in combination with chocolate (above). Light and delicate chocolate mousse, which is traditionally served in individual portions by elegant restaurants, can also presented in a single bowl as a simple country dessert for the whole family (facing page). Some chocolate cakes have become "classics" of modern pastry (following double page), including the Opéra (center); the Sacher torte (center right), and the Feuilles d'automne (top left). Others, like the Paradis (top center), the Pleyel (bottom left), or the Extrême (top right) may be the classics of tomorrow.

once this urge is fulfilled. Deep-rooted habits would be revealed, such as penchants for particular brands or fillings, or the time of day when chocolate is most enjoyed. Statistics could show the proportion of people who eat chocolate before engaging in difficult activities to give themselves courage, and those who eat it afterwards as a well-deserved reward. An amusing paragraph could reveal the ingenious secret hiding-places that people devise in order to be able to enjoy their chocolate in private, far from the curiosity and reproachful glances of their nearest and dearest. Chocoholics would relate their first chocolate experiences, evoke the joys and sorrows of dependence, and describe the lengths to which they will go to procure their daily ration.

The conclusion would concern our relations with our fellow human beings, who alternately tempt, forbid, or share with us. Scholars would explain that chocolate is a language and suggest interpretations enabling us to achieve a better understanding of ourselves and our neighbors. This *magnum opus* would draw to a close with ringing phrases asserting that "chocolate makes you a better person," or, "someone who eats a bar of chocolate a day cannot be all bad." Perhaps the authors would go so far as to paraphrase Descartes and declare, "I eat chocolate therefore I am," or Shakespeare, "to be chocolate or not to be," ending with the metaphysical notion, "tell me about your chocolate and I will tell you who you are."

Almost everyone treasures some tender or melancholy chocolate-related memories; chocolate seems to have been a part of our lives for as far back as we can remember. It constitutes a universal subject, probably because it allows each of us to express ourselves with our hearts, whatever our education, our background, or our past.

Chocolate and the cinema seem to go well together. In this still from the film *Sherlock Jr.*, Buster Keaton seems to be more interested in the pretty salesgirl than in the candies displayed in the store-front window (facing page). This famous scene from George Cukor's 1935 film *Dinner at Eight* shows Jean Harlow as the ultimate *femme fatale*, with her platinum blonde hair, glamorous negligee, satin sheets, heart-shaped pillows, and box of chocolates in Hollywood-style packaging (above).

TRENDS

If there is one thing that unites Europeans, it is certainly their passion for chocolate. Europe alone accounts for nearly 60 percent of worldwide chocolate consumption, twice as much as North America. The average American consumes 10 pounds of chocolate each year, while the average European consumes 12 pounds, although there is a considerable disparity between north and south. Switzerland is in first place with almost 22 pounds of chocolate a year per person, followed by Norway, Austria, and the Netherlands, where each person eats about 18 pounds per year. England, Belgium, Luxembourg, Germany, Ireland, and Sweden are not far behind, with a yearly consumption of close to 15½ pounds per person. France and Finland are gallantly trying to catch up, but their inhabitants cannot seem to manage more than 11 pounds per person per annum. "Choco-mania" is only beginning to take hold in Italy and Spain and, although these two nations are making spectacular progress, for the time being they each attain an annual per capita rate of only 4½ pounds.

What is the reason for this six-to-one difference between the north and the south? First of all, industrial production methods were first developed in Switzerland, Holland, and France and it is therefore logical that consumption tends to be higher in these major chocolate-producing countries. Another reason, which is obvious once you stop to think about it, is that chocolate melts. Before modern refrigeration became widespread, which is, after all, a fairly recent phenomenon, chocolate could not withstand the torrid summers of southern Europe. Since it did not have its place either in children's school bags or on the shelves of rural grocery stores, it never became a staple consumer item.

Whether in hot or cold climates, one thing is certain—the more chocolate people eat, the more they want. The chocolate consumption curve, which has been in constant progression since the 1980s, is quite different from that of other confectionery and sweet products in general. In view of the current world economic crisis, coupled with the glorification of slimness and the condemnation of sugar, it is not surprising that cookies and candy are becoming endangered species. Chocolate, however, seems to be above all that. Every year chocolate consumption progresses steadily, with occasional dramatic leaps, like the increase of no less than 2 pounds per person recorded in the Netherlands during 1991.

Frenzy is perhaps too strong a term, but it is clear that as this century draws to a close chocolate has become a deep-rooted habit that cannot be dismissed as merely a passing fad. Over the past five years, all the European countries have recorded an annual increase in consumption varying from 2 to 5 percent—a trend mirrored in the United States—which clearly indicates an ever-growing interest in chocolate, although different types are more or less appreciated from country to country. In France, for example, sales of assorted chocolate candies are at a standstill or even in regression, while sales of chocolate bars are increasing. The French still prefer the great family of milk chocolate: milk chocolate bars, with or without hazlenuts, crispy rice, or other ingredients,

Chocolate bars inspire great loyalty among chocolate lovers, though personal preferences concerning cocoa content, brand, shape, size, and thickness can vary widely. Some artisan chocolatiers or small-scale manufacturers still start with cacao beans to make their chocolate, including Bonnat in Grenoble, Bernachon in Lyon, Weiss in Saint-Étienne, and Valrhona in Tain-l'Hermitage. The resulting selection is greater and the cocoa content more precise. In addition, the origins of the beans can be indicated. Chocolate bar enthusiasts all agree that once the ideal bar has been found, it is very difficult to change brands (facing page).

"With the sweet fresh air coming up from the garden through the open glass door; to drink, instead of coffee, a cup of chocolate handed on a tray" (Thomas Mann, *Buddenbrooks*). Hot chocolate, which is a natural stimulant, is an excellent mid-afternoon substitute for tea or coffee, especially when it is served with delicate tuiles and florentines (above and facing page). Artisanal chocolates—the highest expression of the chocolatier's art—are currently undergoing an extraordinary revival. The devoted chocolate lover may dream of elaborate silver candy dishes overflowing with the finest chocolates in the world (following double page).

account for more than 50 percent of the market. However, dark chocolate is becoming increasingly popular. Manufacturers of inexpensive bars of dark eating chocolate with a low cocoa content have benefited from the stability of cacao bean prices over the past few years, and these bars now account for 17 percent of the market. Sales of better-quality, *dégustation* bars with a higher cocoa content are reaping the rewards of the aggressive advertising campaigns undertaken by the major producers, and have risen to account for 5 to 7 percent of the market. Dark baking chocolate, which does not always end up in the saucepan or the cake tin, gallantly maintains its position with more than 12 percent of the market, followed closely by a type of high-cocoa-content dark chocolate which specialists call *noir-ingrédient*. The French market can be divided roughly into approximately 40 percent for dark chocolate—which is progressing—50 percent for milk chocolate, and 10 percent for all remaining chocolate-related products combined, including white chocolate and fruit-, cream-, liqueur-, or praline-filled chocolates.

Although current trends seem to indicate that dark chocolate may be the wave of the future, the standardization of tastes and markets is far from being a reality. Consumer habits differ, thankfully, from one country to another. This is due to culture, history, climate, and sometimes religion. In northern Europe, for example, chocolate is considered to be an energy-giving food rather than strictly a candy. It is fully integrated into daily eating habits and is not imbued with any underlying notions of gluttony or sinfulness. The English eat relatively few chocolate bars, but they are extremely fond of sweet chocolate confections, particularly those made with fresh cream, mint, or a unique variety of milk chocolate coating made from liquid milk rather than the dehydrated milk used elsewhere. The Italians are not great consumers of chocolate bars either, but prefer cioccolatini—small, original chocolates which are sold individually. In Spain, the favorites are drinking chocolate and chocolate spread. The Belgians and the Dutch prefer creamy, often fondant-based chocolates, while the celebrated Belgian pralines—retailed by a large network of stores such as Godiva or Léonidas—have their devoted aficionados all over the world. Most Germans are quite incapable of eating dark chocolate with a high cocoa content of 70 percent, which they consider a dietary, or even a medicinal product. Like the French, the Germans adore chocolate bars, preferably on the thin side and made of high-quality milk chocolate. In fact, it is difficult to find any chocolate in Germany with a high percentage of cocoa solids, much to the despair of connoisseurs, who never miss an opportunity to travel to France for supplies. Finally, Americans have a particular taste for soft, chewy chocolate bars filled with caramel, toasted almonds, and, in more sophisticated circles, macadamia nuts.

A Florentine landmark since 1872, the famous Rivoire café, which also has its own brand of fine chocolates, still sells its gianduja chocolate paste accompanied by a small, silver-plated tea spoon (above). In 1860, the celebrated Parisian tea company, Mariage Frères, combined the nutritive properties of superfine chocolate with the digestive virtues of tea (facing page). The result was so successful that the Mariage brothers took out a fifteen-year patent on the recipe. Among the most refined chocolates available are ganaches flavored with different types of tea (green, smoky, or scented) and almost all makers of fine chocolate offer a variety of this elegant confection.

MÉLANGE DU THÈ AVEC LE CHOCOLAT
EARL GREY IMPÉRIAL
MÉLANGE DU THÈ AVEC LE CHOCOLAT
MARCO POLO
MÉLANGE DU THÈ AVEC LE CHOCOLAT
Cloître Saint-Merry, N°4, pres la rue de la Verrerie
CHOCOLAT DES MANDARINS
MÉLANGE DU THÈ AVEC LE CHOCOLAT
Brevete (SGDG)

No one knows how tastes will evolve. The opening of national borders in Europe and large-scale tourism will no doubt result in increased cultural exchanges and new chocolate-eating habits. For the time being, the only factor all these countries have in common is seasonality: more than two-thirds of the annual chocolate production is consumed during the Christmas, New Year, and Easter holidays. Chocolate is still the ideal gift for friends, family, colleagues, and, of course, for ourselves.

TASTE AND COLOR

There can be no unqualified answer to the question of what constitutes "good" chocolate, since matters of taste are, by definition, highly individual. At the most, it can be said that the more varieties of chocolate a connoisseur eats, the more he or she develops a certain discrimination, a sensitivity to the range of flavors, and a number of criteria which form what could be called a "norm," though this term is

In 1937, just a few weeks before Easter, this cheerful employee of the Bedford factory in England and her co-workers were busily preparing traditional chocolate eggs. Hours of hard work and great precision went into the manufacture and decoration of each of these enormous Easter treats (facing page). For many years the production of baking chocolate remained a cottage industry (above).

somewhat out of place. For specialists and assiduous consumers, a good dark chocolate should contain between 55 and 75 percent cocoa solids, the ideal figure being around 60 to 65 percent. It is dark, of course, but with faint red highlights, which are a sign of quality. The aroma is distinctive and rich, almost palpable. The chocolate breaks cleanly, melts rapidly and uniformly in the mouth, and has a complex, long-lasting flavor. Nothing very complicated seems to be involved, at least for the time being! There are those who would like to apply a precise technique and specialized vocabulary to chocolate-tasting, inspired by the ones used by professional wine-tasters. Perhaps in the not-too-distant future, specialist magazines will be peppered with detailed

chocolate-tasting reports, such as "intense, predominantly smoky bouquet, subtle, penetrating, and particularly sensual undertones; homogenous texture, fairly compact, but melting quality, good sugar/acid balance; fruity flavor, with a very long finish and light tobacco and caramel notes—very original"; or perhaps: "a bouquet with cocoa predominating, somewhat classic, faint touches of torrefaction; supple, elastic, and buttery texture; fresh, slightly acid flavor and a moderately long finish with strong notes of vanilla and caramel." For the moment, thank goodness, no one needs to take a course in order to enjoy chocolate, and let us hope that this may always be the case.

Another common misconception is that truly great chocolate must of necessity be dark. Contrary to what chocolate "fundamentalists"—as well as certain advertising agencies—would like us to believe, milk chocolate is just as noble. Consumption of milk chocolate is significantly greater than that of dark chocolate everywhere in the world except France, where milk chocolate is ahead by a mere 10 percent. Perhaps this is because the quality of French dark chocolate has

On 4 April 1828, Coenraad Johannes Van Houten took out a patent for his newly invented cocoa press, which extracted the cocoa butter from the chocolate liquor, leaving behind a "powdery dry substance." Today, powdered cocoa, a Dutch and English specialty, is the basic ingredient of much chocolate-flavored pastry, and confectionery, and many drinks (facing page). Small quantities of pure vanilla (above) are indispensable to the savor of chocolate. Sometimes natural vanilla is replaced by artificial vanilla flavoring, but the quality of the chocolate always suffers.

improved so greatly over the past twenty years. France has also been at the forefront of a quiet revolution in chocolate making. Formerly, the manufacture and sale of fine, artisanal chocolate was a sideline of the pastry shop, the bakery, or the ice cream store. About fifteen years ago, a new profession began to emerge, that of the specialized chocolatier. Today, this new breed of confectioner, who makes handmade, gourmet chocolates according to jealously guarded secret recipes using the finest ingredients, has spread to other parts of the world. Whether in Paris or Lyon, London or Dublin, New York or San Francisco, they are all bursting with creativi-

ty, constantly developing new flavors, new combinations, and new textures.

The taste of a chocolate truffle has, of course, nothing to do with that of a chocolate bar. The main difference lies in the paramount importance of the quality of the enrobing chocolate, whether the truffles are filled with cream, nougat, or liqueur. Chocolate makers sometimes blend as many as four or five types of couverture chocolates, themselves composed of several different varieties of cacoa bean, to create new varieties of enrobing chocolates, which can vary in terms of bitterness, fluidity, and creaminess. Once blended, these must be combined harmo-

Metal confectionery molds were once hammered out by hand, often by the confectioners themselves. Around 1850, tin plate was the standard material used, though today it has been replaced by stainless steel or plastic. Until the Second World War, French craftsmen working in tin plate created an almost infinite variety of imaginatively shaped molds. One of the most famous firms, Ets. Letang, located on rue Vieille-du-Temple in Paris, has over a thousand different models in stock (facing page). Today, only the finest artisanal chocolate makers still use individual molds to produce Easter eggs, chocolate Santa Clauses, and other fanciful subjects.

niously with an infinite number of other ingredients, including butter and cream, the essential components of ganache; almonds and hazlenuts, which are used to make praline, gianduja, and marzipan; as well as brandy, honey, fruit, fondants, and even herbs and spices. The skilled chocolatier then embarks on a fascinating, almost mystical creative endeavor to produce new and unique flavors. This involves utilizing chocolate's numerous chemical properties, compensating for its weaknesses, respecting its character, and anticipating its reactions. Some chocolate makers treat this whole process as a conquest, engaging the raw materials in combat and forcing them to submit to their vision of the world. The resulting chocolates are strong, tempestuous, and excessive, often surprising, and always engaging and charming. Other chocolatiers tame their chocolate gently, listen to it, and mold it to produce confections of apparent simplicity, but which possess exceptional personality and perfect harmony, qualities which everyone who eats them appreciates, but is unable to define. In either case, the chocolates have a mysterious, almost intangible power which makes each mouthful unforgettable and which reveals their creators to be magicians, sorcerers, or alchemists.

These types of artisanal chocolate always deserve the honors of a full tasting ritual, but especially when they are being eaten for the first time. The proper procedure for tasting a ganache begins with an examination of its proportions, regularity of color, and glossy finish—the shape should be harmonious, the highlights deep and reddish. Following this inspection of its exterior, the ganache should be sliced neatly in half with a small, sharp knife, producing a faint crackling sound. The interior should reveal the thin layer of fine enrobing chocolate and the clean texture of the ganache, which should be perfectly creamy and devoid of any visible particles. The aroma should be rich, subtle, and appealing. Now comes the moment of truth, when the ganache is placed in the mouth. The taste should be complex but unified and harmonious: chocolate, of course, is the primary flavor and any additions should only serve to enhance it, not to dominate it. The aftertaste should be strong, but never overpowering, and ideally should stimulate an immediate desire to take another one. The second helping should really be eaten whole, for pleasure alone, without any reflection, this being the only way to form an instinctive, overall impression of the chocolate, and evaluate the appropriateness of its size, the silkiness of its texture, and the harmony of its flavor.

Does it serve any useful purpose to talk about it afterwards, as some connoisseurs recommend? Does analyzing it add to the pleasure? Perhaps the wisest course is to allow people to decide for themselves. Let us simply be grateful for this blissful era in which chocolate tasting is still a simple and joyful experience, devoid of strict guidelines, because this state of affairs may not last for ever. The vogue for chocolate, the emotions it arouses, and the habits and obsessions it engenders, could one day lead to a world in which words like "joy," "sensuality," and "passion" are replaced by standardized chocolate-tasting identification formulae and a vocabulary as pedantic as it is tedious.

The choice of raw materials is of paramount importance in the making of fine chocolate and the names of suppliers are jealously guarded secrets which chocolate makers refuse to divulge under any circumstances. A master chocolatier may import fine Bourbon vanilla from the island of Réunion in the Indian Ocean, rich almonds from Italy or Spain, and lush, dark walnuts from the Dauphiné or the Dordogne regions of France. Products of this quality are rare and expensive, but they make the difference between artisanal and mass-produced chocolate (facing page: Weiss in Saint-Étienne).

WHAT TO DRINK WITH CHOCOLATE

Despite its deceptively simple appearance, chocolate, as we have seen, is a complex delicacy, in which the bitter, the sweet, and the acidic combine to form a confection of unparalled savor. In addition to these three basic components, the intensity and flavor of chocolate can be profoundly influenced by a variety of factors, including texture and subtle aromatic variations. It is therefore impossible to identify the one beverage which would harmonize equally well with a velvety chocolate cake, a chocolate bar containing 70 percent cocoa solids, and a tea-flavored ganache. It is also out of the question to provide precise recommendations, because in order to cover every eventuality, the list would be not only ridiculously long, but, above all, would be impossible to follow. To propose a particular wine, of a particular *appellation*, vintage, and estate, to be drunk at a specific time, place, and temperature, with a unique brand of chocolate might sell a few books, but would serve no useful purpose. The best way to proceed is to follow the simple guidelines outlined below, which are based on combinations of flavors, textures, and chemical reactions.

The rich flavor, complex structure, and temperature-sensitive nature of chocolate makes it difficult to combine with many beverages. However, the taste sensations can be glorious when the taste of chocolate is complemented by the right drink. Topping the list of combinations to avoid is white wine and chocolate, a mismatch that is almost always doomed to failure. Champagne must also be treated with caution; a typical brut champagne is too dry to harmonize with the sweetness of chocolate, although the higher sugar content of a good demi-sec allows it to accompany pralines, truffles, and milk chocolates. Red wines do not bring out the best in chocolate either. This combination is only acceptable at the end of a meal, when a nearly empty glass is crying out to be drunk and there is no other alternative. However, a young, simple, unpretentious red wine, low in tannin, served chilled, can confer a touch of stimulating gaiety to a simple chocolate dessert, though not one made with bitter chocolate. Wines in this category include certain Beaujolais, Bordeaux and red wines from the Loire Valley. One should be prudent, however, with a fine Bordeaux, especially one that is young, because the tannins naturally present in the wine, supplemented by the oak tannins from the barrels, will fight with the tannins of the chocolate, creating a mouthful so bitter that it often provokes grimaces. Strangely enough, some people seem to adore this combination, which is certainly virile, to put it mildly. A subdued red wine is not really acceptable either, because the strong taste of the chocolate dominates the mild flavor of the wine, leading to an experience without glory or pleasure.

Strong, fruity white wines like Chablis or Sancerre have the opposite disadvantage; they mask the subtle aromas of the chocolate and prevent it from developing its full flavor. Chocolate takes its revenge by accentuating the somewhat thick consistency of the wine, making it seem heavy and utterly without grace. It is best to avoid this weak, sugary, and decidedly uninteresting encounter, in which the faults of both are resolved by a sort of double suicide. Only an excellent, "late-harvested" Alsace Gewürztraminer can

Chocolate all its guises—bars, truffles, pralines, or squares—is even more irresistible when accompanied by fine brandies, such as cognac and armagnac, or grain-based liquors like whisky and bourbon. If the alcohols are at least ten to fifteen years old and of irreproachable quality, their flavor when combined with chocolate is remarkable. For particularly rare and expensive varieties, small glass marbles can be added to the bottle to diminish evaporation by reducing the surface area of the liquid. With a moist or particularly rich chocolate cake, a younger brandy diluted with very pure water is an unusual but delicious taste sensation.

occasionally accompany a bittersweet dark chocolate with mild success, lending it a fleeting, refreshing, aromatic touch, even if the combination is often somewhat simplistic. There is nothing particularly praiseworthy in this useless sacrifice of a good bottle of wine, which certainly deserves a better end.

In the absence of a satisfactory solution, some chocolate lovers turn to cold water. Between two mouthfuls, between two chocolates, water quenches the thirst and cleanses the palate. Fresh water is the faithful ally of the professional chocolate taster, but its very neutrality precludes it from providing any particular pleasure for the amateur chocolate lover.

The same cannot be said for coffee, which is recognized throughout the world as one of the most successful beverages to drink with chocolate. Coffee and chocolate are, in fact, radically different. While chocolate blends graciously with a great number of other ingredients, including spices, fruit, and even aromatic herbs and plants, the possibilities of coffee are more limited, though these include vanilla and, as it happens, chocolate. Many chocolatiers add a barely perceptible drop of coffee extract to their ganaches or truffles, which enhances the chocolate flavor. The love story between coffee and chocolate should be placed among the world's great flavor combinations, ranging from the coffee *crème anglaise* which is served with many chocolate desserts, to mocha-flavored cakes, ice creams, and hot chocolate. At

the end of a meal, coffee is the best choice a chocolate lover can make. The robust taste of the strong, hot coffee brings out all the flavor of a chocolate dessert, while a square of sophisticated dark chocolate, dipped in the coffee cup, is a delight which is enjoyed by coffee and chocolate aficionados alike.

Aside from coffee, there are only two other types of beverage with which chocolate can be eaten successfully: fortified wines such as sherry, and fruit-based eaux-de-vie; and spirits which have been aged for a long time in oak barrels, such as cognac and whiskey. These families provide an extraordinary range of taste sensations when combined with chocolate. Certain fortified wines from the Roussillon region in southwestern France, such as wines from the Banyuls, Maury, and Rivesaltes *appellations*, have a flavor that complements that of chocolate remarkably well. The combination, which was first proposed by a handful of Parisian sommeliers during the 1970s, has gradually spread to the best restaurants in France and around the world. These deeply colored, mysterious wines, with their notes of dried fruits, spices, burnt wood, coffee, or caramel, seem to have been created to go with chocolate. Their tannins blend with those of the chocolate, neither masking the other, to create a subtle harmony, which is both delicate and powerful. The other wines in the same family are also delicious with chocolate, like a fine, twenty-year-old vintage port, a cream sherry aged in oak, a great madeira,

Serving a square piece of chocolate with coffee after a meal was originally an Italian custom, but during the 1980s this delightful idea caught on throughout the world. At first, the chocolate served was a Neapolitan, a small, fairly thick rectangle of rather ordinary chocolate. Today, the square is rivaled by a variety of chocolate-coated "coffee beans," ranging from caramelized almonds rolled in cocoa powder to real roasted coffee beans dipped in dark chocolate. The small glass pictured here contains chocolate liqueur, which was very much in fashion before the war (facing page). The flavor of this warm chocolate tart (above) may be enhanced by a touch of coffee.

unfortunately so rare outside its native island, a Marco de Bartoli Marsala, or the exotic and bewitching Corvo Ala, with its unusual pistachio notes, both from Sicily.

Brandies, liqueurs, and spirits all have a privileged relationship with chocolate in its guises. In order to harmonize with chocolate, various wine-based brandies like cognac or armagnac, fruit-based liqueurs like eau-de-vie or calvados, and grain-based whiskies or bourbons, have to be aged patiently in oak barrels. The aging process is what imparts the amber tones, and the powerful notes of vanilla, dried flowers, or exotic wood. These complex flavors bring out all the subtlety of chocolate—particularly if the cocoa content is high—when the alcohol is drunk in small sips between each mouthful. While all of these varieties go remarkably well with chocolate, the best results are obtained with fifteen- to twenty-five-year-old armagnacs, or with equally mature, single malt whiskies. With a cake, a mousse, or a soufflé, a young, five- or six-year-old cognac diluted with very pure, chilled mineral water is an excellent choice. The result is an aromatic, thirst-quenching beverage, which goes wonderfully well with the frothy or creamy textures of the chocolate desserts without ever overpowering them. The affinities of chocolate with fruit or nuts take on new dimensions when oranges, hazelnuts, or almonds are replaced by Grand Marnier, Fra Angelico, or Amaretto.

To conclude on a note of pure fantasy, the Conticini brothers, who run the Table d'Anvers restaurant in Paris, concoct their own astounding *parfums à boire* by infusing ginger, citronella, cinnamon, liquorice, and sugar, which they serve with fine chocolate; the possibilities are endless. Chocolate, judiciously named the "food of the gods," will continue to surprise and enchant us lesser mortals until the end of time.

The harmony between chocolate and fortified wines stems from a chemical reaction between the two substances. This is due not so much to the high sugar content of the wine, but rather to the aromatic complexity it develops from being aged in oak barrels. Notes of roasted almonds, candied fruit, or toasted bread wonderfully enhance the flavors of fruit- and nut-filled chocolates, palets d'or, and truffles (facing page). Sweet biscuits, like the delicate ladyfingers used to make this homemade charlotte (above), and freshly baked French specialties, like the chocolate-covered brioche on the following page, are the perfect foils for appreciating the quality of fine baking chocolates.

FAVORITE
CHOCOLATE
RECIPES

C*hocolate can be prepared in an infinite variety of ways. However, many recipes using chocolate are often complicated and require specialized ingredients, kitchen equipment, and cooking skills. We have selected a collection of chocolate recipes that are easy to follow and even easier to eat, which can be made and enjoyed by the entire family for many years to come. When the recipes call for bittersweet chocolate, we recommend using one with a minimum of 55% cocoa solids.*

CAKE AU CHOCOLAT

The French use the word "cake" to refer to what Americans call a sweet tea bread. This recipe was created by Jean-Luc Poujauran, one of the finest bakers in Paris. The simple, family-style loaf is delicious fresh out of the oven and also keeps well for several days, although this is rarely necessary!

INGREDIENTS	2½ TABLESPOONS (30 G)
FOR 6 SERVINGS	COCOA POWDER
2 EGGS, SEPARATED	¼ CUP (60 G) SWEET
½ CUP (100 G)	BUTTER
ALL-PURPOSE FLOUR	¼ CUP (60 G) HEAVY CREAM
⅛ CUP (35 G) BROWN SUGAR	PINCH OF SALT
1 TEASPOON BAKING POWDER	

Cream the butter and brown sugar in a mixing bowl until light and fluffy.
Add the egg yolks one by one, mixing well after each addition.
Sift together the flour, cocoa powder, baking powder, and salt. Stir gently into the egg mixture with a wooden spoon alternately with the heavy cream, beginning and ending with the dry ingredients.
Whip the egg whites with a pinch of salt until stiff and fold them into the batter.
Pour the batter gently into a small buttered and floured loaf pan and bake at 320°F (160°C) for 35 minutes, or until a knife inserted into the center comes out clean.

HOT CHOCOLATE

Lovers of hot chocolate appreciate both its taste and texture. The flavor can be varied by using a delicate blend of different types of chocolate. As for the texture, there is only one solution: take a wire whisk and beat, beat, and beat again! In this classic French recipe, the hot chocolate is prepared without sugar, which can be added to individual cups according to taste.

INGREDIENTS	1 CUP (25 CL) LIGHT CREAM
FOR 8 SERVINGS	½ VANILLA BEAN
8 OZ (200 G) BITTERSWEET	1½ TABLESPOONS (20 G)
CHOCOLATE	COCOA POWDER
3⅛ CUPS (75 CL) MILK	

Break the chocolate into small pieces.
Pour the milk and the cream into a small heavy saucepan and add the vanilla bean, split lengthwise, and the cocoa powder. Stir well and bring to a boil.
Remove from heat and cool by placing the pan into a bowl of cold water. Add the chocolate, and stir until it is melted.
Reheat the mixture over a low flame (but do not boil) for 5 minutes, stirring constantly with a wooden spoon so it does not stick.
Remove the vanilla bean. Whisk the hot chocolate just before serving until it is foamy. Serve with a dollop of fresh whipped cream sprinkled with unsweetened cocoa powder.

CHOCOLATE TRUFFLES

Truffles are among the easiest chocolate confections to make. Once the cream and the chocolate have been combined, the children can take over the rest, which they love to do. The flavor can be varied by adding a ¼ cup of Grand Marnier, rum, brandy, fruit liqueur, or other alcohol to the ganache filling.

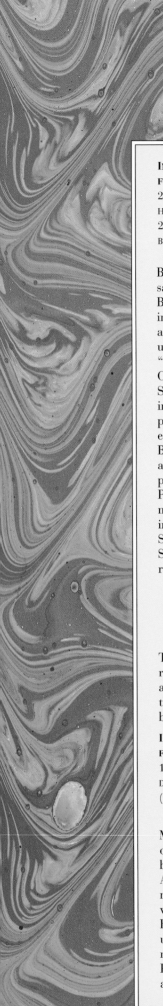

INGREDIENTS
FOR AROUND 70 TRUFFLES
2¼ CUPS (500 G)
HEAVY CREAM
26½ OZ (750 G)
BITTERSWEET CHOCOLATE
2 OZ (50 G) BITTER
CHOCOLATE
1⅛ CUPS (250 G)
POWDERED UNSWEETENED
COCOA

Bring the cream to a boil in a small heavy saucepan.

Break 21 oz. (600 g) of the bittersweet chocolate into small pieces, place in a heat-resistant bowl, and pour the hot cream over it, stirring constantly until well blended and smooth (this forms the "ganache" filling).

Cover and refrigerate until firm, about 2 hours.

Scoop up the ganache with a teaspoon and shape into individual balls by rolling the mixture in the palm of the hand. Put the balls back in the refrigerator for a few minutes.

Break up the rest of the bittersweet chocolate along with the bitter chocolate and melt in the top part of a double boiler set over simmering water.

Place each truffle on a fork, plunge it into the melted chocolate, pull it out immediately, and roll in the cocoa powder.

Shake off the excess cocoa powder and set aside. Store keep the truffles in a cool place, but do not refrigerate.

WILLI'S WINE BAR
DARK CHOCOLATE TERRINE

The fame of this intimate Parisian wine bar resides in the quality of the fabulous wine list, and the remarkable dark chocolate terrine. Dense, thick, and rich, it is delicious when accompanied by a lightly sweetened crème anglaise.

INGREDIENTS
FOR 6 SERVINGS
18 OZ (500 G)
DARK BITTER CHOCOLATE
(70% COCOA SOLIDS)
1⅓ CUPS (300 G)
SWEET BUTTER
6 EGGS, SEPARATED
PLUS 1 EGG WHITE
PINCH OF SALT

Melt the chocolate with the butter in the top of a double boiler. Stir well and transfer to a mixing bowl to cool.

Add the 6 egg yolks to the warm, but not hot melted chocolate and butter one at a time, mixing well after each addition.

Beat the seven egg whites with a pinch of salt until stiff, and fold them gently into the chocolate mixture.

Pour into a loaf pan and refrigerate, covered, for at least 12 hours.

BUTTER GANACHE

Ganache is a mixture of chocolate and cream, usually with some butter added, that is used as a filling for chocolate cakes and other desserts, as well as for numerous chocolate confections. Many recipes for ganache exist, but this one is the easiest and the most reliable. More butter can be added to make the ganache creamier and more fluid, depending on how you plan to use it.

INGREDIENTS
8 OZ (200 G) BITTERSWEET
CHOCOLATE
1 CUP (200 G) HEAVY
CREAM, PREFERABLY
UNPASTURIZED
3 TABLESPOONS (25 G)
SWEET BUTTER

Break the chocolate into small pieces and place in a heat-resistant bowl. Heat the cream in a small heavy saucepan. When it boils, pour the cream over the chocolate, stirring constantly until it is melted. Add the butter and mix until very smooth and well blended.

Gradually add a small amount of warm water while mixing until the desired consistency is obtained. If necessary, reheat in the top part of a double boiler when ready to use.

CHOCOLATE CAKE

A classic chocolate cake recipe which continues to delight. For a creamy, tender texture, place the cake tin on a rack in a pan of warm water for baking, as for a custard. The cake is also delicious baked in the traditional manner.

INGREDIENTS
FOR 6 SERVINGS
14 OZ (400 G)
BITTERSWEET CHOCOLATE
6 EGGS, SEPARATED
½ CUP (110 G) GRANULATED
SUGAR
1 CUP (200 G) SWEET
BUTTER, SOFTENED
⅛ CUP (35 G) ALL-PURPOSE
FLOUR
PINCH OF SALT

Break the chocolate into small pieces and melt slowly in the top of a double boiler set over simmering water.

Butter and flour a 10-inch springform pan (or a round cake pan if using the custard method). Preheat oven to 390°F (200°C).

Beat the egg yolks with the sugar until thick and pale yellow.

Stir the softened butter into the chocolate and fold into the egg mixture. Fold in the flour.

Beat the egg whites with a pinch of salt until firm and fold gently into the batter.

Pour the batter into the prepared cake pan and bake for 45 minutes to an hour, or until a cake tester inserted in the center comes out clean. Allow to cool completely before removing from pan and sprinkle with confectioner's sugar before serving, if desired.

TARTE FINE AU CHOCOLAT

This chocolate pie with an ultra-thin crust is a French specialty that first became popular during the 1980s. The crust is a classic pâte brisée, and the thinner it is the better. The recipe calls for removing the lightly cooked crust from the pan before filling, but this is a very delicate operation and the pie will be just as delicious served from the pan.

INGREDIENTS
FOR 6 SERVINGS
FOR THE PATE BRISÉE:
1 CUP (200 G) ALL-PURPOSE FLOUR
½ CUP (100 G) SWEET BUTTER, SOFTENED
2 EGG YOLKS
PINCH OF SALT
3 TABLESPOONS COLD WATER

FOR THE CHOCOLATE FILLING:
9 OZ (250 G) BITTERSWEET CHOCOLATE
⅔ CUP (150 G) LIGHT CREAM
½ VANILLA BEAN
2 EGG YOLKS
2½ TABLESPOONS (30 G) SWEET BUTTER, SOFTENED

To make the pâte brisée:
Sift the flour and the salt into a mixing bowl, making a well in the center. Place the cold water, the egg yolks, and the butter in small pieces, into the well and knead gently until the dough becomes workable. Turn the dough out onto a work surface and, using the palm of the hand, push the dough away from you to blend the ingredients thoroughly. Gather the dough into a ball, wrap in a damp cloth or plastic wrap, and refrigerate for at least an hour.
Heat the oven to 390°F (200°C).
Unwrap the chilled dough and roll it out to a thickness of ⅛ inch (3 mm) on a floured work surface. Place the dough into a buttered pie or tart pan and pat it well into place. Prick the bottom with a fork. Line the pan with foil or wax paper, fill with dry beans to weight it down, and bake until the crust starts to color, about 10 minutes. Remove the lining and the beans and bake for about 5 minutes more, or until the crust turns a light golden brown; the crust should be lightly cooked. Remove from the oven and let cool. Carefully remove the crust, which will be very fragile, from the pan and place it on a rack.

Break the chocolate into small pieces and place in a large, heat-resistant mixing bowl.
Heat the cream with the vanilla bean, split lengthwise. When the cream begins to boil, remove the vanilla bean and pour the cream over the chocolate. Stir well, until the chocolate melts and the mixture is well blended and smooth. Add the egg yolks and the softened butter and mix well.
Pour the still-warm filling into the lightly cooked pie crust and cool completely before serving.

BROWNIES

Brownies, the classic American dessert, today have conquered the world. Even the most sophisticated European gourmets have to admit that the nut and chocolate combination is irresistible. Try replacing the walnuts with pecans to vary the flavor.

INGREDIENTS
FOR SIX SERVINGS
5 OZ (150 G) BITTER CHOCOLATE
⅓ CUP (80 G) SWEET BUTTER
2 EGGS
1 TEASPOON VANILLA EXTRACT

⅔ CUP (150 G) GRANULATED SUGAR
½ CUP (100 G) ALL-PURPOSE FLOUR
½ TEASPOON BAKING POWDER
½ CUP (100 G) COARSELY CHOPPED WALNUTS

Preheat the oven to 350°F (180°C). Butter and flour a 8 x 8 inch (20 cm) square baking pan.
Melt the butter and chocolate together in the top of a double boiler. When melted, set aside to cool. Beat the eggs and the sugar until thick and light yellow and add the vanilla. Fold the chocolate and butter into the eggs and sugar and mix thoroughly. Sift the flour with the baking powder and fold gently into the batter, mixing until just blended. Fold in the walnuts.
Pour the batter into the prepared pan and bake for 25 to 30 minutes or until the center is just set. Allow to cool before cutting into squares.

CHOCOLATE MOUSSE

More or less sugar, more or less butter or heavy cream . . . with chocolate mousse, the possibilities are endless. This classic recipe is rich but not too sweet, and can be varied by the addition of orange zest, crystallized ginger, or a dash of brandy or fruit liqueurs. A prudent blend of different brands of chocolate can add an unexpected dimension.

INGREDIENTS
FOR 6 SERVINGS
8 OZ (200 G) BITTERSWEET
CHOCOLATE
⅔ CUP (150 G) HEAVY
CREAM

¼ CUP (50 G) BUTTER
5 EGGS, SEPARATED
⅛ CUP (30 G) GRANULATED
SUGAR
PINCH OF SALT

Break the chocolate into small pieces and place in a heat-resistant mixing bowl. Heat the cream in a small saucepan and bring to a boil. Pour the hot cream over the chocolate and mix until the chocolate melts. Add the butter and mix well (add a dash of liquor or alcohol, if desired).
Add the egg yolks one by one, mixing well after each addition. Let cool to room temperature.
Beat the egg whites with a pinch of salt until they are very firm. Continue beating and gradually add the sugar.
Add a third of the egg whites to the chocolate and mix carefully. Then gently fold the remaining egg whites into the chocolate mixture. Pour into a serving bowl or individual dessert cups. Refrigerate for at least 12 hours before serving.

CHOCOLATE PUDDING

This is a simple, comforting dessert which brings back memories of childhood. Many of us grew up on pre-packaged chocolate pudding mix, but this recipe is as simple to make and just as infallible.

INGREDIENTS
FOR SIX SERVINGS
8 OZ (200 G) BITTERSWEET
CHOCOLATE
3 CUPS (75 CL) WHOLE MILK
6 EGGS, SEPARATED

⅓ CUP (80 G) GRANULATED
SUGAR
3 TABLESPOONS (40 G)
CORNSTARCH

Serve this thick, creamy, homemade pudding with ladyfingers or whipped cream and you will taste the difference.
Break the chocolate into small pieces and place in a heat-resistant bowl
Heat 2¾ cups (65 cl) of the milk in a heavy saucepan. When it comes to a boil pour the hot milk over the chocolate and stir until melted.
Dissolve the cornstarch in ¼ cup (10 cl) of milk. Beat the sugar and the egg yolks in a large mixing bowl until light yellow. Stir in the cornstarch. Slowly pour the hot milk and chocolate over the egg mixture.
Return the mixture to the saucepan and bring to a low boil for 2 minutes, stirring constantly until it thickens. Pour into a serving bowl or individual cups through a fine sieve or cheesecloth and refrigerate. Serve cold.

CHOCOLATE SAUCE

This simple, versatile sauce can be used for profiteroles, ice cream sundaes, or as an excellent substitute for store-bought syrups or powders to make chocolate milk.

INGREDIENTS FOR SIX
SERVINGS
8 OZ (200 G) BITTERSWEET

CHOCOLATE
½ CUP (100 G) HEAVY
CREAM

Break the chocolate into small pieces and place in a heat-resistant bowl. Heat the heavy cream. When the cream boils, pour it over the chocolate and stir until melted. Gradually add a small quantity of warm water until the sauce achieves the desired consistency. If necessary, reheat in a double boiler before using.

CONNOISSEUR'S GUIDE

CHOCOLATIERS AND CHOCOLATE SHOPS
UNITED STATES AND CANADA

BALDUCCI'S
424 Sixth Avenue, New York, NY 11011
Tel.: 212 673-2600
Mail Order: 1-800 BALDUCCI
Established in 1948, Balducci's food emporium offers a sumptuous selection of chocolates and chocolate cakes. The fillings are exceptional, with surprising festive flavors such as pumpkin, eggnog, whisky, and maple syrup. House specialties include Chocolate Velvet Mousse Cake and Chocolate Ribbon Cake.

BLACK HOUND NEW YORK
170 Second Avenue, New York, NY 10003
Tel.: 212 979-9505
Mail Order: 1-800 344-4417
www.blackhoundny.com
Elegantly simple Shaker-style boxes contain Black Hound's premier all-natural truffles, made by hand in small batches with a taste and look reminiscent of early America. Rustic hand-woven baskets are filled with assorted truffles, dark chocolate bark, and bittersweet nut clusters. Also available are rich chocolate cakes, tortes, and cookies made from all-natural ingredients.

BERNARD CALLEBAUT CHOCOLATERIE
1313 1st Street S.E., Calgary, AB T2G 5L1, Canada. Tel.: 1-800 661-8367
www.bernardcallebaut.com
Bernard Callebaut, from the fourth generation of Belgian chocolatiers, brought his family tradition to Calgary, Alberta, in 1982. Known for his wide variety of nearly 70 different centers, including 20 different seasonal flavors, Callebaut has established his presence in North America with 21 stores in Canada, one in Seattle, Washington, and mail order throughout the United States. With the focus on holiday gifts, packaging ranges from chocolate egg and heart-shaped boxes to hand-painted ceramics from Portugal. Don't miss the chocolate-covered cherries.

ORTRUD MÜNCH CARSTENS
Gotham Gardens, 325 75th Street, New York, NY 10023. Tel.: 212 877-8908
The use of the freshest, finest ingredients combined with the purest cocoa make this one of the best chocolate shops to be found in New York City. Whether it be Earl Grey tea flown in from Paris or fresh fruit from the West Coast, every ingredient is excellent. But it is the superb Valrhona couverture that ensures perfection. As for creativity, Ortrud Carstens gives her imagination free rein with sculptured or molded works of art, such as her "rusty tools" collection. Her chocolates are also available from Mad 61 and Manhattan Fruiterer in New York, and from Dean & Deluca in both New York and Washington DC.

LE CHOCOLATIER
1840 North East 164 Street, North Miami Beach, FL 33312. Tel.: 305 944-3020
Nancy Jehlen first opened this small chocolate shop in 1980. It quickly became well known for the exceptional quality of its confections and in 1986 was sold to Joseph Marmor and the German-trained chocolatier Baruch Schaked. House specialties include Grand Marnier truffles, and a line of kosher chocolates.

DILETTANTE CHOCOLATES
Pike Place Market, 1603 1st Avenue, Seattle, WA 98101. Tel.: 206 728-9144
www.dilettante.com
The Davenports have inherited recipes passed down through three generations from the pastry chef of Russia's Czar Nicolas II. Their award-winning sauces and topping include Truffle Topping, Chocolate Fondue, and Caramelized Cream Ice Cream Topping.

RICHARD DONNELLY FINE CHOCOLATES
1509 Mission Street, Santa Cruz, CA 95060
Tel.: 1-888 685-1871
www.donnellychocolates.com
Donnelly's reputation is built on his bite-sized solid chocolate bars wrapped in gold foil and Japanese rice paper of rich colors such as malachite, onyx, and ruby. The flavors are equally distinctive: dark chocolate with ginger, almond, or orange; milk chocolate hazelnut; and almond toffee.

FRAN'S CHOCOLATES
1300 East Pike Street, Seattle, WA 98122-0452
Tel.: 206 322-0233
Fran Bigelow is probably the best overall chocolatier in the United States, making truffles, pralines, and elaborate butter-cream cakes. Fran's technique is impeccable, and her sense of taste both lush and subtle. The truffles and pralines are available by mail order, but not the classic cakes and tortes, which are alone worth a trip to Seattle.

GHIRARDELLI PREMIUM CHOCOLATES
900 North Point Street, San Francisco, CA 94109.
Tel.: 415 474-3938. www.ghirardelli.com
Domenico Ghirardelli started his career by providing groceries for the rush of gold prospectors. In 1852 he established the California Chocolate Manufactory, which quickly became a thriving business. The renovated Ghirardelli Square factory is still a landmark for visitors, who can watch chocolate being made the old-fashioned way and then stock up on Ghirardelli Bittersweet Chocolate and Unsweetered Cocoa.

GODIVA CHOCOLATIER
793 Madison Avenue, New York, NY 10021
Tel.: 212 249-9444
Almost 20 years ago Godiva Chocolatier introduced its Belgian-style bonbons to America, single-handedly creating the demand for luxury chocolates.

The carefully crafted shell heightens the fine flavor made possible by superior ingredients. From its famous truffles to sculptures of solid chocolate, from sleek molded pieces filled with such luscious centers as hazelnut praline, almond butter, marzipan, raspberry butter cream, and mandarin orange to its new Petites, Godiva is committed to excellence in the Belgian tradition. The success of the boutique on Fifth Avenue in New York City has led to the opening of over 115 boutiques in the United States, with many others worldwide (see also Godiva Belgium and United Kingdom).

HARBOR SWEETS
Palmer Cove, 85 Leavitt Street, Salem, MA 01970.
Tel.: 617 745-7648 or 1-800 243-2115
A former executive at a large Boston candy company, Benneville Strohecker started making chocolates in his kitchen offering flexible hours to part-time workers—a haven for young mothers and retired people. Harbor Sweets is best known for chocolates in nautical forms, such as the caramel-filled Sand dollar, peppermint Marblehead Mint, chocolate Barque Sarah, or sailboat-shaped Sweet Sloop—all named after boats from the 1850s. The Sweet Sloop, which accounts for half of Harbor Sweets' sales, is a butter crunch of toasted pecans dipped in dark chocolate with white chocolate decoration. The sugar content in all of their candies is lower, and the cocoa solids higher, than in most commercial brands.

LA MAISON DU CHOCOLAT
1018 Madison Avenue, New York, NY 10021
Tel.: 212 744-7117
www.lamaisonduchocolat.com
First established in 1977 in a former wine cellar on rue du Faubourg-Saint-Honoré by internationally celebrated chocolatier Robert Linxe, three additional boutiques have since opened in Paris and one in New York. Recognized as the finest master chocolatier in the world, hailed by gourmet chefs, and supplier to the most sophisticated connoisseurs, Robert Linxe has remained a traditional craftsman as well as an artist. The New York boutique of La Maison du Chocolat organizes tastings and seminars.

MATISSE CHOCOLATIER
260 Grand Avenue, Englewood, NJ 07631
Tel.: 201 568-2288
www.matissechocolatier.com
With the intimacy that only a small business can offer, the staff at Matisse works closely with customers to determine their specific needs. Choose from a complete luxury assortment of handmade truffles, caramels, dipped fresh fruits, or sculptured solids to be enjoyed individually or in any of the unique baskets imported from all over the world.

PERUGINA
370 Market Street, Saddle Brook, NJ 67801
Tel.: 201 843-4200 or 1-800 745-6199
www.nestleeuropeanchocolate.com/perugina

Perugina was named after the Italian town of the founder Pepino Buitoni. Since its American introduction at the New York World's Fair in 1939, Perugina has become the largest importer of fine boxed chocolates in the United States. Much of Perugina's history is graced with legend, from the romantic Baci chocolate kisses to the fabled Griffin guarding Perugina's exquisite confections. Made with only the choicest premium quality products—hazelnuts, almonds, and cherries, from the best Italian harvests—Perugina offers individually wrapped candies such as the famous Baci, and an assortment of fine chocolate bars among its counter items, as well as a selection of elegant gift boxes.

PETERBROOKE CHOCOLATIER

2024 San Marco Blvd., Jacksonville, FL 32207
Tel.: 904 398-2488 or 1-800 771-0019
Peterbrooke practices the art of dipping a variety of foods in chocolate. Fruits, nuts, cookies, pretzels, popcorn, and even whole apples are hand dipped into the tempered chocolate made in each of the four Florida locations. A whimsically clever "chocolate pizza" of milk chocolate presented in an authentic pizza delivery box topped with fruits and nuts can be ordered and delivered to your doorstep.

RICHART DESIGN ET CHOCOLAT

7 East 55th Street, New York, NY 10022
Mail Order: 1-888 RICHART
www.richart-chocolates.com
Established in 1925 in Lyon, France, the Richard family practises their own unique art of chocolate, combining aesthetics, innovation, and exceptional quality. Each boutique is a "chocolate gallery" and serves as a place where both amateurs and connoisseurs meet to experience the pleasures of chocolate. Attractive sculpted chocolates are fashioned in a variety of presentations for all kinds of people, from the athlete to the music lover. The richly elegant dessert sculptures present the ultimate grand finale.

JOSEPH SCHMIDT CONFECTIONS

3489 16th Street, San Francisco. CA 94114
Tel.: 415 861-8682
www2.mailordercentral.com/jschmidtconfections
Opened in 1983 by Joseph Schmidt and Audrey Ryan, Joseph Schmidt Confections has been honored with national art shows and counts many celebrities among its clients. Schmidt, of Austrian heritage, was trained as a pastry chef but soon turned to chocolate as the ideal means to express his boundless creativity. His sculptural works range from a miniature version of a San Francisco cable car, which was presented to Queen Elizabeth II, to an Eiffel Tower, made for the French ambassador. But his chocolates are not only for looking at, they are also delicious to eat. Made with fine Callebaut couverture from Belgium, the well-balanced ingredients are never too sweet or too cloying.

RUSSELL STOVER CANDIES

625 South Colorado Boulevard, Denver,
CO 80246. Tel.: 303 744-9425
www.russellstover.com
Dedicated to making assorted boxed chocolates, Russell Stover Candies has grown spectacularly over the past 30 years, developing from a small regional company to the nation's largest. The company likes to say that the same care, quality, and ingredients go into every box of candy today as did in the Stover bungalow back in 1923. The product line includes a variety for every customer, occasion, and price range. There are currently 48 Russell Stover retail stores throughout the United States, as well as two in Canada.

TOUCAN CHOCOLATES

Mail order address: P.O. Box72, Waban, MA 02168
Tel.: 617 964-3696 or 1-800 816-8696
Toucan Chocolates grew out of Michael and Susan Goldman's commitment to the environment and their love of fine chocolates. The tastes and textures of tropical nuts are melded with the world's best milk and dark chocolates to create assortments of four, ten, and twenty pieces. Each variety—including cashew-caramel tortoises, nut-chocolate clusters, nut caramels, cashew bark, and Brazil-nut butter crunch—is packaged in specially designed biodegradable, recycled paper containers. Part of the proceeds from each box goes to Cultural Survival, Inc. for their work in helping inhabitants of tropical forest regions.

WHITMAN'S CANDIES

4900 Oak Street, Kansas City, MO 64113
Tel.: 816 471-1669
Purchased and distributed by Russell Stover Candies since 1993, Whitman's still maintains its place in American chocolate history. Stephen F. Whitman first founded his confectionery in 1842 on the Philadelphia wharf to compete with French candy makers. He kept fruits and nuts on hand so that customers could order their own custom-made assortment. This eventually led, in 1912, to the Whitman Sampler with its famous "cross-stitched" packaging and index to the chocolates. The original box now belongs to the Philadelphia Museum of Art. Continuing to make both boxed chocolate and candy bars. Whitman's have recently launched Lite Chocolates, with approximately 40 calories per candy.

GREAT BRITAIN

ACKERMANS

9 Goldhurst Terrace, Swiss Cottage, London NW6
3HX. Tel.: 020 7624 2742
Started over 50 years ago in a shop on Goldhurst Terrace, Ackermans was awarded the Royal Warrant in 1969. The present master chocolatier is German-born Franz Hippel whose specialties include Swiss recipe truffles in classic flavors such as champagne, whisky, cognac, and rum. Other house specialties include Easter eggs. Valentine hearts, Christmas figures, crocodiles, and champagne bottles filled with Marc de Champagne Truffles. They are available at leading department stores and fine grocery stores, as well as by mail order through the Chocolate Club (see listing below under Clubs).

BENDICKS OF MAYFAIR

Moorside Road, Winchester, Hampshire SO23 7SA
Tel.: 01962 844800. www.bendicks.co.uk
Bendicks was founded in 1921 as a pastry shop and confectioner, but the chocolate was such a success that the pastry business was soon abandoned. Bendicks' most famous creation is the Bittermint, a creamy mint fondant made from pure peppermint oil, enrobed with unsweetened chocolate. In 1962 Bendicks was given a Royal Warrant by Queen Elizabeth II. Other house specialties include: the Creme de Menthe, a bittersweet chocolate filled with a green mint fondant; the Mint Crisp, mint-flavored chocolate sprinkled with crunchy honeycomb; Chocolate Peppermint Creams, and White Chocolate Mints. An assortment is packaged in an elegant cream and gold embossed box perfect for gift-giving.

CHARBONNEL ET WALKER

The Royal Arcade, 28 Old Bond Street, London
WIX 3AB. Tel.: 020 7493 6768
Under the arcades of the elegant candy-colored passageway opening onto Old Bond Street, this firm, which has held a Royal Warrant since 1875, does much to reconcile the British with the continental taste for dark chocolate. However, the packaging and the rose, violet, and geranium creams are typically English. Other chocolates are filled with whisky, rum, cognac, or champagne. Do not leave the premises without a box of powder to make hot chocolate or a pot of truffle sauce for covering crêpes and ice cream.

FORTNUM & MASON

181 Piccadilly, London W1A 1ER
Tel.: 020 7734 8040
www.fortnumandmason.com
In 1707 William Fortnum and Hugh Mason became partners in what started out as a grocery store providing the fashionable St. James's neighborhood with new and exotic products. Chocolate became one such item and in the 1920s Fortnum & Mason established a confectionery department that produced its own chocolate. They soon became famous for their fondants, hand-dipped nuts, brandied cherries, caramels, nougats, and marzipan that are still part of what is called their Superb Selection. Other house specialties include Rose and Violet Creams, Royal Liqueurs, Champagne Truffles, and Elegant Thins.

GODIVA

141 Regent Street, London W1B 4JA
Tel.: 020 7734 8113. www.godiva.com
This giant Belgian-chocolate empire was founded in 1929 by the Draps family. In London the house specialties include Dame Blanche, Truffle Amere, Cerisette, Truffle Fine Champagne, and Carré Godiva. The moiré-silk boxes are beautifully crafted to make an exquisite gift.

HARRODS

87-135 Brompton Road, Knightsbridge, London
SW1X 7XL. Tel.: 020 7730 1234
www.harrods.com
The confectionery department of Harrods' distinguished food hall (established 1849) offers a sumptuous selection of handmade chocolates from traditional British names such as Terry's of York, Bendicks of Mayfair, or Rowntree, along with classic Belgian chocolates including Godiva and Léonidas. Harrods also features fine chocolates from the exceptional master chocolatiers Gerard Ronay and Joseph Schmidt.

MELCHOIR CHOCOLATES
Station Road, South Molton, Devon EX36 3LL
Tel.: 01769 574442
www.melchiorchocolates.co.uk
What started out in 1977 as small batches of chocolates to serve with coffee in his seaside restaurant soon grew into full-time chocolate-making for Swiss-born Carol Melchoir. House specialties include fruit and liqueur truffles; personalized chocolate logos; and seasonal themes. Available at Fortnum & Mason and other specialized stores as well as by mail order worldwide.

MONTGOMERY MOORE
Unit D Blenheim House, Blenheim Road,
Longmead Business Park, Epsom, Surrey KT19
9AP. Tel.: 01372 742597
www.montgomerymoore.co.uk
Starting from a French couverture with a very high cocoa content, Montgomery Moore creams are filled with typically British flavors, such as violet, ginger, or tea. Don't leave the shop without a bottle of the house's hot chocolate. Montgomery Moore chocolates can also be purchased at The Conran Shop or at Selfridge's on Oxford Street, which, after Harrods, is the second largest department store in London.

PRESTAT
14 Princes Arcade, Piccadilly, London SW1Y 6DS.
Tel.: 020 7629 4838. www.prestat.co.uk
Truffles enrobed with powdered cocoa in round or log form are made with a secret family recipe that dates back to the time of Napoleon III. The Prestat chocolate company was first established on Oxford Street in 1902 and continues to hold a Royal Warrant although it has gone through several takeovers and changes of location. Other than their famous truffles, specialties include the Connoisseur Assortment and Brandy Cherries.

ROCOCO
321 King's Road, London SW3 5EP
Tel.: 020 7352 5857. www.rococochocolates.com
Tucked among the trendy boutiques of London's Kings Road you'll find this small shop that Chantal Coady has filled with a treasure-trove of chocolate bonbons. The truffles are made from a very strong criollo bean, while bars with distinctive notes of tea, juniper, thyme, and lavender will satisfy connoisseurs of strong, fruity dark chocolate. The traditional English hand-dipped chocolates have fillings, which include such classics as geranium, raspberry, and coffee cream. Rococo chocolates can also be purchased at The Conran Shop.

SANDRINE CHOCOLATES
239 Upper Richmond Road West, London SW14
8QS. Tel.: 0208 878 8168. www.sandrine.co.uk
Sandrine offers Christmas boxes of handmade, Belgian-style chocolates with fillings including fondants, marzipan, praline, and fresh creams. Retail at the shop; wholesale by telephone.

THORNTONS
Outlets throughout the U.K. and Ireland
Tel.: 0800 454 537 (UK only) or 0845 1211911
www.thorntons.co.uk

Makers of hand-crafted chocolates and confections, Thorntons are already famous for their Continental Selection. They now offer a Continental French Selection for lovers of dark chocolate. Call the above number for store addresses.

IRELAND

BUTLERS IRISH
Clonshaugh Industrial Estate, Dublin 17
Tel.: 353-1 6710599. www.butlerschocolates.com
These luscious Irish chocolates are available at the above address and through most fine supermarkets and delicatessens.

CADBURY IRELAND, LTD.
Coslock, Dublin 5
Tel.: 353-1 8480000. www.cadbury.ie
Founded by the Quakers in the early nineteenth century, Cadbury is the most celebrated chocolate manufacturer in the U.K. (see also the listings Museums).

LÉONIDAS
Royal Hibernian Way, Dawson Street, Dublin 2
Tel.: 353-1 6795915. www.leonidas.com
Léonidas has a number of stores selling the celebrated Belgian brand of hallmark fine chocolates. The firm has six stores in Dublin alone and outlets in most major towns.

LIR CHOCOLATE
421 IDA Enterprise Centre, East Wall Road,
Dublin 3 Tel.: 353-1 8740365. www.lirchocolates.ie
Manufacturers of delectable handmade chocolates.

FRANCE – PARIS

CACAO ET CHOCOLAT
63 Rue St-Louis en l'Isle, 75004 Paris
Tel.: 01 46 33 33 33
29 Rue de Buci, 75006 Paris
Tel.: 01 46 33 77 63
36 Rue Vieille du Temple, 75004 Paris
Tel.: 01 42 71 50 06
In these ultra-modern boutiques, you will find the chili and honey chocolates made famous by the film *Chocolate*, delicate ganaches flavored with fruit and spices, as well as chocolate Aztec masks.

MICHEL CHAUDUN
149 Rue de l'Université, 75007 Paris
Tel.: 01 47 53 74 40
The delicious window displays of this great chocolate master draw Parisian gourmands, some of whom would go nowhere else to buy their chocolates. With 70 % cocoa and fragments of roasted nib, Colomb delights unconditional lovers of pure chocolate, as does Esmeralda, a bitter chocolate truffle. Grenade, a milk truffle, and Haiti, a sumptuous caramel mousse, are much sweeter without being cloying.

CHRISTIAN CONSTANT
46 Rue de l'Université, 75006 Paris
Tel.: 01 47 03 30 00
37 Rue d'Assas, 75007 Paris
Tel.: 01 53 63 15 15
www.christianconstant.com

A few tables are provided for improvised tasting of Orangettes, a highly colorful marriage of dark chocolate and crystallized mandarin peel from Sicily; sublime ganaches flavored with just a hint of vanilla, vervain, jasmine, or cardamom; or bitter truffles. But Christian Constant is also a great *pâtissier* and we advise you to taste the Orpheo Negro (chocolate and raspberry) or the Soleil Noir (a dome of bitter chocolate mousse flavored with cinnamon).

DALLOYAU
101 Rue du Faubourg-Saint-Honoré,
75008 Paris. Tel.: 01 42 99 90 00
2 Place Édmond-Rostand, 75006 Paris
Tel.: 01 43 29 31 10. www.dalloyau.fr
You will love the chocolate macaroons at this Paris *pâtissier*-chocolatier, where you can also taste a Mogador (chocolate and raspberries) or purchase chips to prepare creamy hot chocolate at home.

DEBAUVE ET GALLAIS
30 Rue des Saints-Pères, 75007 Paris.
Tel.: 01 45 48 54 67
33 Rue Vivienne, 75002 Paris.
Tel.: 01 40 39 05 50
www.debauve-et-gallais.com
Among the mouth-watering chocolates available, one unusual gift is an assortment of Pistoles de Marie-Antoinette, which are filled with double vanilla, almond milk, orgeat cream, coffee, and orange flower. Also delicious are the grilled Arabica coffee beans covered with chocolate.

DENISE ACABO / A L'ETOILE D'OR
30 Rue Fontaine, 75009 Paris
Tel.: 01 48 74 59 55
Denise Acabo is famous in the world of chocolate. Hers is the only place in Paris where you can find the specialties of Bernard Dufoux and Bernachon among a wide choice of the best products from the greatest chocolatiers.

FOUQUET
22 Rue François-1er, 75008 Paris
Tel.: 01 47 23 30 36
36, rue Laffitte, 75009 Paris
Tel.: 01 47 70 85 00
www.fouquet.fr
Fouquet's is located almost at the corner of Avenue Montaigne next to the Caron perfume boutique. The décor of this venerable family establishment has changed little since it opened in 1852, nor have the traditional production methods. The bitter dark chocolate (72 or 85 %) is one of the fine house specialties.

JADIS ET GOURMANDE
49 bis Avenue Franklin-Roosevelt, 75004 Paris
Tel.: 01 42 25 06 04
39 Rue des Archives, 75003 Paris
Tel.: 01 48 04 08 03
88 Boulevard du Port-Royal, 75013 Paris
Tel.: 01 43 26 17 75
27 Rue du Boissy-d'Anglas, 75008 Paris
Tel.: 01 42 65 23 23
Two delightful specialties are the Tresses à l'Orange (crystallized oranges, bitter chocolate, almonds, and nougat) decorated with holly leaves

for Advent; and the Chapeau d'Orange, partly enro-bed with a thin coating of dark chocolate and thick layers of gianduja, being much less expensive than classic gianduja. The proprietor, Istvan d'Eliassy, will compose the merriest of messages for you with dark chocolate letters placed on a praline and gian-duja base. He can also design shapes to your taste.

LENOTRE

44 Rue d'Auteuil, 75016 Paris
Tel.: 01 45 24 52 52
15 Boulevard de Courcelles, 75008 Paris
Tel.: 01 45 63 87 63
61 Rue Lecourbe, 75015 Paris
Tel.: 01 42 73 20 97
48 Avenue Victor Hugo, 75016 Paris
Tel.: 01 45 02 21 21
121 Avenue de Wagram, 75017 Paris
Tel.: 01 47 63 70 30
www.lenotre.com
Croquants or fondants, light and fragrant truffles, rich ganaches with tenacious flavors— Lenôtre chocolates live up to their reputation. Our favorite was the Palet Lenôtre, a particularly bitter *palet d'or* in a dark chocolate shell. Of the irresistible cakes, our preferences were the Meringue d'Automne and the Côte d'Ivoire. Lenôtre has so many shops in Paris that inquiries should be addressed to the above.

LA MAISON DU CHOCOLAT

225 Rue du Faubourg-Saint-Honoré,
75008 Paris. Tel.: 01 42 27 39 44
52 Rue François-1er, 75008 Paris
Tel.: 01 47 23 38 25
19 Rue de Sèvre, 75006 Paris
Tel.: 01 45 44 20 40
8 Boulevard de la Madeleine, 75009 Paris
Tel.: 01 47 42 86 52
89 Avenue Raymond-Poincaré, 75016 Paris
Tel.: 01 40 67 77 83
www.lamaisonduchocolat.com
Impossible to choose among the ganaches perfected by the grand master chocolatier Robert Linxe: wrap-ped in an extremely fine coating, they are superbly light. You can savor the pure chocolate of Quito, Caracas, or Guayaquil, then partake of the flavors of Otello, Andalousie (fresh lemon), Maïko (ginger), Zagora (mint), or Garrigua (fennel).

LA MARQUISE DE SÉVIGNÉ

32 Place de la Madeleine, 75008 Paris
Tel.: 01 42 65 19 47
1 Place Victor-Hugo, 75016 Paris
Tel.: 01 45 00 89 68
These two Meccas of Parisian chocolate have managed to keep a somewhat old-fashioned charm. Lined up in elegant boxes are Amandes Princesse (Majorca almonds grilled and caramel-ized then enrobed with chocolate), Cœur de Paris (filled with hazelnuts or hazelnut praline) and Palets Amer Café.

PIERRE MAUDUIT

54 Rue du Faubourg-St-Denis, 75010 Paris
Tel.: 01 42 46 45 64
12 Boulevard de Denain, 75010 Paris
Tel.: 01 48 78 05 30

This is the place to find gorgeous boxes of choco-late shavings with a high percentage of cacao. Perfect for making a good hot chocolate or for sprinkling on buttered bread at tea-time.

À LA MERE DE FAMILLE

35 Rue du Faubourg-Montmartre, 75009 Paris
Tel.: 01 47 70 83 69
One of the prettiest boutiques to be found in Paris, this specialty grocery store holds treasures that will enchant the connoisseur. Products of the finest choc-olatiers sit side by side with lovely glass jars that pre-ciously conserve the house creations.

A LA PETITE FABRIQUE

12 Rue Saint-Sabin, 75011 Paris
Tel.: 01 48 05 82 02
Jean Rambaud's workshop behind the Opéra-Bastille is a veritable chocolate factory. With a bit of luck you will be able to watch him at work. Among his wonderful creations are truffles and *palets d'or*.

FRANCE – PROVINCES

BERNACHON

42 Cours Franklin-Roosevelt, 69006 Lyon
Tel.: 04 78 24 37 98. www.bernachon.com
"Bernachon is obviously one of the most visited Lyon monuments. And the most appreciated, since you come back... happiness already in your eyes and on your tongue," wrote the popular French TV perso-nality, Bernard Pivot. The great specialty of Maurice and Jean-Jacques Bernachon are their *palets d'or*. Do not leave the premises without stopping in the tea room for a hot chocolate or slice of cake; we recom-mend the sumptuous President topped with a rustle of fine chocolate shavings and created by the famous chef Paul Bocuse and Maurice Bernachon.

YVON BERTHELOT

1 Place de l'Hôtel-de-Ville, 60400 Noyon
Tel.: 03 44 44 02 56
This chocolatier founded his reputation not only on the quality of his "Muscadines," the orange and praline ganaches that are his town's specialty, but also on his fabulous collection of ancient molds in steel, silver-plated copper, and tin-plated iron.

BONNAT

8 Cours Senozan, 38500 Voiron
Tel.: 04 76 05 28 09
www.bonnat-chocolatier.com
Raymond Bonnat was the first to think of using wine terms such as "cru" for rating chocolates and speaks of Chuao, made with Venezuelan beans, as if he were talking about a bottle of Romanée-Conti. The old-fashioned display shelves offer pyramids of multicolored candies; an assortment of Pavés de Voiron (almond and hazelnut pralines); chocolates with Chartreuse liqueur (the monastery being nearby); and locally gathered walnuts on a gian-duja base enrobed with strong dark chocolate.

AU DUC DE PRASLIN

Place Mirabeau, 45200 Montargis
Tel.: 02 38 98 63 55
125 Avenue Victor-Hugo, 75016 Paris
Tel.: 01 44 05 18 08

It is to the Duke of Plessis-Praslin that we owe the appellation "praline." Originally the term was used for the grilled almonds offered by the duke to Louis XIII. The recipe concocted by his "palate" officer founded the glory of the Confiserie du Roy at Montargis and continues to be a house specialty today. Other delights include almonds enrobed with chocolate and powdered like truffles, and ganaches flavored with pineapple, white rum, or ginger.

BERNARD DUFOUX

32 Rue Centrale, 71800 La Clayette
Tel.: 03 85 28 28 10. www.chocolatsdufour.com
La Clayette, in the heart of Burgundy not far from Roanne, is an obligatory stop due to the presence of Bernard Dufoux. This master chocolatier *extraordinaire* prepares ganaches with every flavor imaginable—wild blackberry, raspberry, fresh mint—as well as those that you would never ima-gine: Indian spices, mace, Jamaican red pepper (to eat as an aperitif). Our preferences were Green (made from fresh green leaves) and Badiane. But Bernard Dufoux can also create more traditional marvels such as the exquisite Caprice de Caroline (a praline of caramel, truffle, and fresh pistachio) or the Palais Bourbon (with Bourbon vanilla).

JOËL DURAND

3 bd Victor-Hugo, Saint-rémy-de-Provence
Tel.: 04 90 92 38 25
Like all great chocolatiers, Joël Durand pushes his passion to the limit. While some of his flavors are surprising, even disturbing, his ganaches— Earl Grey, cinnamon, lavender, enrobed with airy choco-late—place him among the best French chocolatiers. He is also a renowned *pâtissier*.

KOENIG

11 Rue Pasteur, 57000 Metz
Tel.: 0387 66 71 48
20 Nouvelle Rue, 57000 Metz
Tel.: 03 87 36 72 72
42 Rue des Dominicains, 54000 Nancy
Tel.: 03 87 36 72 72
www.chocolats-koenig.com
All of Pierre Koenig's chocolates are of artisanal fabrication. His specialties are whisky truffles; almond slices with bitter dark chocolate; *palets d'or* (bitter ganache with a touch of coffee fra-grance); and Amandine (praline mousse presented in a very thin crispy shell).

LEROUX

18 Rue du Port-Maria, 56170 Quiberon
Tel.: 02 97 50 06 83. www.chocolatleroux.com
From subtle buckwheat or mint tea ganaches to extraordinary chocolate caramels, Henri Leroux makes the best chocolates in Brittany. When in sea-son, he uses fresh Périgord truffles to flavor his bitter chocolate ones. His coffee beans, enrobed in chocolate then sprinkled with cocoa powder have less than five calories each, and are a delight for weight-watchers.

RICHART

1 Rue du Plat, 69002 Lyon
Tel.: 04 78 37 38 55
258 Boulevard Saint-Germain, 75007 Paris
Tel.: 01 45 55 66 00. www.richart.com

The slogan "design et chocolat" hints at what one can expect here. In these immaculate halls dedicated to cacao, chocolates are exhibited like art works in a gallery, smooth and shiny, silk-screened with colored chocolate, and packaged in clever gift boxes with drawers.

WEISS

8 Rue du Général-Foy, 42000 Saint-Étienne
Tel.: 04 77 32 41 80. www.chocolat-weiss.fr
A traditional house founded in 1882, Weiss is one of the great names in chocolate. While the production facilities and the original boutique with its antique décor are found in Saint-Étienne, other shops have been opened in Lyon, Paris, Roanne, and Toulouse. The firm is perhaps less known for its chocolate bonbons than for its bars and Neapolitans.

AUSTRIA

ALTMANN & KÜHNE

30 Graben, 1010 Vienna. Tel.: 1 533 09 27
For nearly a hundred years these doll-sized bonbons have been made with the same natural, preservative-free ingredients. House specialties include miniature chocolates, nougat with rum, fondants, and chocolate coffee beans, packaged in whimsical boxes such as a miniature treasure chest or a tiny chest of drawers. Available at the Vienna shop or by mail order.

BELGIUM

GODIVA

22 Grand-Place, Brussels
Tel.: 2 511 2537. www.godiva.com
Purveyors by special appointment to the Belgian court, it is only natural that Godiva be located on the Grand-Place, although there are several other stores throughout the city. You can taste milk chocolates filled with orange praline and crushed hazelnuts; dark chocolate filled with a milk chocolate paste and orange cream; white chocolate with a praline filling and crunchy sugar decoration. Chocolates for this store and for distribution throughout Europe are made in Belgium, while a factory in Pennsylvania supplies the American market (see Godiva listing under United States and United Kingdom).

LÉONIDAS

46 Boulevard Anspach, Brussels
Tel.: 2 218 0363. www.leonidas.com
The pralines are among the creamiest and sweetest to be found in Belgium. The Manon made with fresh cream was one of the first pralines to be enrobed with white chocolate rather than melted sugar. Another Léonidas innovation was to replace the traditional walnut center by a grilled hazelnut. Besides the above address, Léonidas has three other shops in Brussels.

MARY

73 Rue Royale, Brussels 1000
Tel.: 2 217 4500. www.marychoc.com
In a royal blue décor that does not hesitate to mix Italian rococo with Louis XVI, this purveyor by special appointment to the Belgian court makes 70 different sorts of chocolate, mainly dark. Some of the recipes date back to end of the last century; but others are more recent, such as the famous Astrid, invented for the princess of the same name, or Ephémère, a dark chocolate with fresh cream, made only for the winter season.

NEUHAUS

25-27 Galeries de la Reine, Brussels
Tel.: 2 502 5914
www.neuhauschocolate.com
The "queen's gallery," an elegant passage that ends up on the Grand-Place, is a most agreeable place to wander about. Since 1857 Neuhaus has been the area's gourmet attraction. Jean Neuhaus is said to be the inventor of the Belgian praline and in spite of the fact that the fine confectionery is now a multinational business, certain pralines, such as the Manon, are still handmade.

WITTAMER

6 Place du Grand Sablon, 1000 Brussels
Tel.: 2 512 3742. www.wittamer.com
Founded in 1910, this famous pastry shop-chocolatier is located in the Grand Sablon neighborhood, a center for the antiques trade. In 1984 a separate confectionery was opened and it now offers some 65 pralines, a dozen of which are excellent. Filled with fresh cream, flavors include pistachio, Grand Marnier, pineapple, and raspberry. Do not pass up the Trianon, filled with buttery cream and nougat, or the Bouchon with Grand Marnier.

ITALY

MAJANI

5 Via dei Carbonesi, Bologna
Tel.: 51 234 302. www.majanichocolate.com
Majani, the oldest Italian confectioner's shop, dates from 1834: the tea room of this prosperous business was visited by Napoleon III himself. In a décor of antique furniture and crystal containers, let yourself be temped by the chocolate Scorza (bark) and the Fiat Cremino. This chewy cube, made of alternating layers of chocolate with almonds or with hazelnuts, was created in 1911 in honor of the new Fiat Tipo. While the original Tipo is no longer on the road, the Fiat chocolate still has fans who will choose it over every other gianduja. Don't even try to resist the Gianduja Ingot, which melts so easily it can only be sold in winter; it is cut with a knife and sold by weight.

PEYRANO

47 Corso Moncalieri, Turin
Tel.: 11 660 2202
76 Corso Vittorio Emanuele II, Turin
Tel.: 11 562 3072
One of the members of the very small club of master chocolatiers who grind their own cacao beans, Giorgio Peyrano produces one of the best chocolates that exist in his tiny laboratory on the Corso Moncalieri. The same choice of fresh chocolates can be found in the shop under the arcades of Corso Vittorio Emanuele II, near the train station. Be warned: you will not be allowed to leave the city without buying Peyrano's giandujas. The town's honor depends upon it. In addition, it is one of the rare places (perhaps the only) where you can buy a jar of *bicerin* paste, a mixture of chocolate and honey used to sweeten coffee—an original gift to bring home for friends.

SWITZERLAND

BEELER

29 Spitalgasse, Berne. Tel.: 31 311 2808
Under the arcades in the center of the city is one of the best Swiss chocolate boutiques where freshness is the golden rule. All of the truffles, especially those with champagne, are sublime. Be sure not to miss the Caramelina, filled with a caramel ganache.

CHOCOLATERIE MICHELI

1 Rue Micheli-du-Crest, Geneva. Tel.: 22 329 9006
For 30 years Pierre Poncioni has devoted himself to bitter chocolate. He has created dark chocolate bars with 75 % and 85 % cocoa, but he is most famous for a 100 % cocoa bar, which is a brilliant success considering that it does not contain one gram of sugar. His charming old-fashioned shop doubles as a tea room: take the time to enjoy a delicious cup of hot chocolate.

SPRÜNGLI

Paradeplatz, Zurich. Tel.: 1 224 4711
www.spruengli.ch
Not to be confused with the firm that makes chocolate bars (belonging to a cousin). This Sprüngli draws chocolate lovers for its Truffes du Jour, truffles made fresh each day. But its choice of chocolate bonbons is equally varied and delicious.

TSCHIRREN

73 Kramgasse, Berne. Tel.: 31 311 1717
It is said that Philippe Suchard created his first chocolates in this establishment. Located in the heart of the old town, the shop was taken over by the Tschirren family in 1919 and has since become a chocolate-lover's landmark. Give in to the tempting truffles, whether fruit-filled— prune, apricot, mandarin—or flavored with champagne, cognac, or even honey and rum.

CHOCOLATE BY THE CUP OR SLICE

NEW YORK

CAFÉ LALO

201 West 83rd Street, New York, NY 10024
Tel.: 212 496-6031
A chocolate cake for every mood plus other scrumptious desserts and coffees draw New Yorkers to this atmospheric West Side café.

CAFFÈ VIVALDI

32 Jones Street, New York, NY 10013
Tel.: 212 691-7538 or 929-9384
An idyllic Greenwich Village café with a European ambiance that specializes in classic desserts and classical music. Come in the winter and sit by the fireside.

FERRARA
195 Grand Street, New York, NY 10013
Tel.: 212 226-6150. www.ferraracafe.com
A cafe does not stay in business for over a hundred years, as Ferrara has, without doing something right. The forte of this Little Italy landmark is the cappuccino and Italian pastries.

KAFFEEHAUS
131 Eighth Avenue, New York, NY 10003
Tel.: 212 229-9702
It may be in Chelsea, but the sumptuous desserts and coffee have an air of Vienna about them. The food in this stylish, newly opened "coffeeteria" is not only delicious but attractively priced.

RUMPLEMAYER'S
St. Moritz Hotel, 50 Central Park South,
New York, NY 10019. Tel.: 212 446-5525
Austrian-born Antoine Rumplemayer founded his family business in Nice in 1870. Angelina, the wife of his son René, gave her name to the famous *salon de chocolat* which was established in Paris in 1903, while in New York the name Rumplemayer became synonymous with delicious hot chocolate. For generations cosmopolitans have delighted in the elegant porcelain chocolate services, while their children have been charmed by the enormous collection of stuffed toy animals that greet them at the entrance.

SERENDIPITY 3
225 East 60th Street, New York. NY 10022
Tel.: 212 838-3531
www.serendipity3.com
This combination ice-cream parlor and toy exhibition for kids of all ages offers colossal desserts, including their own bizarre, but intriguing, frozen hot chocolate.

VENIERO
342 East 11th Street, New York, NY 10003
Tel.: 212 674-7070. www.venierospastry.com
The "grandfather" of all other New York pastry shop-coffee houses, this century-old East Village monument stays well in advance of the competition from the trendy new cafés. Its Italian pastries *gelati*, espresso and cappuccino are classics.

LONDON

BROWN'S
Albermarle and Dover Streets, London W1S 4BP.
Tel.: 020 7493 6020
www.brownshotel.com
One of London's oldest and most traditional hotels serves now-legendary afternoon teas—including chocolate cakes, pastries, and biscuits—in the lounge, decorated in classic English chintz. Waiters in tail coats bring you silver tiered cake-stands loaded with delights.

THE DORCHESTER
53 Park Lane, London W1A 2HJ
Tel.: 020 729 8888. www.dorchesterhotel.com
Afternoon tea at the elegant Dorchester hotel is a tradition. Served in the flower-decked Promenade, the offerings are a delight for chocolate lovers, and indeed for everyone.

FORTNUM & MASON
181 Piccadilly, London W1A IER
Tel.: 020 7734 8040.
www.fortnumandmason.com
Fortnum and Mason is renowned for its range of exotic foods—it reputedly used to sell chocolate-covered ants! Delicious hot chocolate as well as cakes and other chocolate delicacies are served at each of the three restaurants in the Piccadilly store—The Fountain, The Patio and The Saint James's. The latter also provides an elegant setting for high tea, taken to the accompaniment of a pianist.

HARRODS
87–135 Brompton Road, London SW1X 7XL
Tel.: 020 7730 1234. www.harrods.com
The restaurants located within the food halls offer a wide range of chocolate delights, including pastries, beverages, and cakes.

PARIS

ANGELINA
226 Rue de Rivoli, Paris 75001
Tel.: 01 42 60 82 00
www.angelina.fr
Every hot chocolate connoisseur knows this tea room located under the arcades opposite the Tuileries Gardens. Rich, fragrant, and extremely thick, the African chocolate is served boiling hot with a glass of water and a bowl of whipped cream. Its recipe is jealously guarded; we only know that it is cooked for a very long time in 8-gallon copper pots. In the shop at the entrance to the tea room you can buy chocolate in packets for preparing delicious beverages at home.

LA CHARLOTTE DE L'ISLE
24 Rue Saint-Louis-en-l'Isle, 75004 Paris
Tel.: 01 43 54 25 83
This little tea room on the Ile Saint-Louis has faithful customers who appreciate the old-fashioned décor, the original cakes, and the collection of chocolate molds.

LADURÉE
16, rue Royale, 75008 Paris
Tel.: 01 42 60 21 79
75 Avenue des Champs-Élysées, 75008 Paris
Tel.: 01 40 75 08 75
21 Rue Bonaparte, 75006 Paris
Tel.: 01 44 07 64 87
www.laduree.fr
Temples to the macaroon, these elegant tea rooms, decorated in 19th century style with painted ceilings, offer a very wide selection of chocolate pastries that have rightly earned an excellent reputation. One fine example is the *Symphonie Noire*, a cacao biscuit with thin chocolate leaves made from a Madagascan cru. You can also taste a chocolate simply called the 75 Champs-Élysées!

L'HEURE GOURMANDE
22 Passage Dauphine, 75006 Paris
Tel.: 01 46 34 00 40
Two types of hot chocolate are served in this small tea room. The *chocolat viennois* served with whip-ped cream and a glass of water, or the long-brewed *chocolat à l'ancienne*. Both are prepared with Valrhona chocolate.

LE MEURICE
228 Rue de Rivoli, 75001 Paris
Tel.: 01 44 58 10 10. www.meuricehotel.com
Nothing equals a steaming hot chocolate served with brioche, gingerbread, or macaroons in one of the most beautiful Paris hotels. The menu, which resembles the finest wine list, is a dream in itself. And there is nothing wrong with lingering over the description when deciding between the delights of Manjari's "slightly tart bouquet with raspberry and strawberry notes" or the "harmonious savor of dry fruits and woody accents" of the Grand Cru des Caraïbes.

CAFÉ RICHELIEU
Place du Carrousel, 75001 Paris
Tel.: 01 47 03 99 68
Located on the first floor of the Louvre's Richelieu wing, this tea room has a very modern décor by Jean-Michel Wilmotte with a faïence ceiling by Jean-Pierre Raymond. The unbelievably creamy hot chocolate *à l'ancienne* is served with cinnamon and whipped cream.

AUSTRIA

CAFÉ IMPERIAL
16 Kärtner Ring, Vienna. Tel.: 1 501 10389
This café reflects the tradition and elegance of the hotel established in the former palace of the Duke of Württemberg, with the motto "Reside, eat, and live like princes." The milk chocolate Imperial torte, which rivals the Sacher torte, is sent by mail order throughout the world.

DEMEL
14 Kohlmarkt, Vienna. Tel.: 1 535 1717
At the height of Austrian-Hungarian pastry shops, the rococo interiors seemed to be covered with as much sugar and icing as the cakes. The windows of this marvelous place are legendary and its atmosphere brings back Vienna at the height of its glory. The café's Eduard Sacher Torte has a strong following. Contrary to the famous torte from the Hotel Sacher, the thin layer of apricot jam is placed just under the icing, not in the middle of the cake itself.

GERSTNER
11-15 Kärtnerstrasse, Vienna. Tel.: 1 512 4963
Purveyors to the imperial court since 1847 and renowned master confectioners, this combined pastry shop, café, and restaurant is very popular with the people of Vienna. Gerstner also supplies buffets for the Vienna Opera.

HEINER
9 Wollzeile, Vienna. Tel.: 1 512 2343
Another supplier to the court, established since 1870, "the Heiner" as it is called by the locals, has nothing pretentious about its decoration, but it is very well known for pastries and hot chocolate.

SACHER

4 Philharmonikestrasse, Vienna 1010
Tel.: 1 51 456 899
The marble, paneling, and mirrors of the café have all the charm of the Hotel Sacher, a monument of Viennese hospitality. At the entrance, gourmands wait patiently in line to buy the legendary Sacher torte (packaged in a wooden box) that Greta Garbo claimed to eat with "no guilt at all."

ZAUNER

7 Pfarrgasse, Bad Ischl
Tel.: 6132 233 1020. www.zauner.at
Since 1832, one of the most prestigious café-pastry shops in Austria and Europe has been located in the small town where Emperor Franz Joseph spent his summers. The old-fashioned display of cakes in the windows is irresistible. Zauner mails its specialties throughout the world.

GERMANY

ANDERSEN

153 Wansbeker Markstrasse, Hamburg
Tel.: 40 68 94 64. www.café-andersen.de
Pastry chefs from father to son, the Andersens have been established in Hamburg for three generations. Their café-cum-pastry shop is among the city's gastronomic centers. The Sacher torte, pralines, and truffles are tantalizing.

KÖNIG

12 Lichtentaler Strasse Baden-Baden
Tel.: 7221 235 73
Pâtissier and art connoisseur (he owns one of the largest private collections of the work of Joseph Beuys), Alfred Greisinger is respectful of traditions. Chocolate lovers visit this gastronomic center of Baden-Baden, decorated with Chippendale furniture, to enjoy a hot chocolate prepared "as it should be" and served on a silver platter.

KRANZLER

18 Kurfürstendamm, Berlin
Tel.: 30 882 6911
Johann Georg Kranzler's café is a must. Its Biedermeier décor, with old faïence stoves, pictures of Berlin in bygone days, and Prussian porcelain provide a wonderful setting for savoring enormous tortes, ice cream, and hot chocolate. Pralines are prepared according to Swiss recipes and decorated with Berlin motifs.

ITALY

AL BICERIN

5 Piazza della Consolata, Turin
Tel.: (11) 463 9325
Since 1763 the façade of this small café has brightened up one of the prettiest squares of Turin. Eight marble pedestal tables, simple wood paneling, and jars of bonbons provide a dream setting for tasting a *bicerin*, the half coffee, half hot chocolate specialty of Turin.

RIVOIRE

5r Piazza della Signoria, Florence
Tel.: (55) 214 412
On this magnificent square, a veritable sculpture garden, the Rivoire café is one of the most pleasant spots of the city. Here, you can taste a savory hot chocolate, buy bars of chocolate wrapped in brightly colored paper, and for lovers of very sweet chocolate, enjoy the *crema cioccolato*, a chocolate cream that comes with its own spoon in a red velvet box.

CHOCOLATE CLUBS AND ASSOCIATIONS

CHOCOLATE LOVERS CLUB

c/o *Chocolatier*, Dept. A 92, PO Box 333;
Mt Morris, IL 61054
Chocolatier, a bimonthly magazine for gourmet chocolate lovers, offers its subscribers membership of the Chocolate Lovers Club, which allows them discounts on the confections offered in the monthly bulletin.

CHOCOLATE MANUFACTURERS ASSOCIATION OF THE USA

8320 Old Courthouse Road, Suite 300, Vienna, VA 22181. Tel.: 703 790-5011
www.chocolateusa.org
An organization of American chocolate companies that conducts surveys and publishes reports about the fluctuations of the chocolate industry in America. Nearly all the major U.S. chocolate makers are represented, including Hershey Foods Corporation, M&M/Mars, and the Nestle Company Inc.

THE CHOCOLATE SOCIETY

Clay Pit Lane, Roecliffe, North Yorkshire
Tel.: 1423 322230. www.chocolate.co.uk
Founded in 1991, this association already has over three thousand members, many of them gastronomy professionals. In addition to Valrhona products, The Chocolate Society offers its members Norwood House Chocolate, which is specially produced in its own chocolate factory. These products are also available from fine British chocolate shops such as Fortnum and Mason in London. Every two months members receive a newsletter which includes book reviews, chocolate gossip, and an agenda of upcoming events such as chocolate tasting with master chocolatiers including Robert Linxe.

LE CLUB DES CROQUEURS DE CHOCOLAT

11 bis, rue de la Planche, 75007 Paris
www.croqueurschocolat.com
This club meets four or five times a year to taste cakes and chocolates, then deliver the results of their investigations in a small but excellent work, *Le Guide des Croqueurs de chocolat*, edited by Claude Lebey. A certificate is awarded to the best artisan; the master chocolatiers Robert Linxe (Paris) and Gerard Ronay (London) have both received the honor. Membership in the club, which is limited to 150, is controlled by a strict sponsorship policy.

MUSEUMS

CADBURY

Linden Road, Bournville, Birmingham, England
Tel.: 0121 451 4180. www.cadburyworld.co.uk
The model village of Bournville, originally constructed to provide an ideal setting for Cadbury factory workers, is now a theme park. A museum showing life in a chocolate factory, a replica of an old-time chocolate shop, and a film recounting Cadbury's history introduce visitors to the story of chocolate-making in Britain.

CANDY AMERICANA MUSEUM

Wilbur Chocolate's Factory Candy Outlet, Lititz, PA. Tel.: 1-888 2WILBUR
www.wilburbuds.com/docs/museum
A candy kitchen from the 1900s exhibits utensils, molds, porcelain chocolate pots, and all sorts of paraphernalia used by early American confectioners to satisfy the growing demand for chocolate.

HERSHEY CHOCOLATE USA

170 West Hershey Park Drive, Hershey, PA 17033. Tel.: 717 534-3439
www.hersheymuseum.org
Milton Hershey started his career producing caramel but eventually decided that chocolate would be the candy of the twentieth century. He sold his million-dollar caramel factory and built a chocolate plant and model town. Besides tours that take visitors through the chocolate process from cacao bean to Hershey Bar, Hershey's also runs a yearly Great American Chocolate Festival.

IMHOFF-STOLLWERCK MUSEUM

Rheinauhafen, Cologne, Germany
Tel.: 221 931-8880. www.schokoladenmuseum.de
Cologne's Imhoff-Stollwerck empire, which has been producing chocolate since 1860, has become even richer with an excellent museum. In addition to demonstrating the cultivation of cacao beans and the history of chocolate-making, it also displays an assortment of utensils, porcelain chocolate pots, posters, and an amazing collection of antique chocolate vending machines. Visitors can also watch chocolate being made.

MUSÉE JACQUES

16 Rue de l'Industrie, B-4700 Eupen, Belgium
Tel.: 087 59 29 29. www.chocojacques.be
Here you can discover the history of cocoa production and watch chocolate actually being made. The porcelain and silver on display evoke the ceremony that surrounded early chocolate-tasting sessions.

SCHOKO-LAND

Alprose-The World of Chocolate
6987 Caslano-Lugano, Switzerland
Tel.: 091 611 8856
In the heart of Tessin, the Alprose firm has set up the first and only chocolate museum in Switzerland. A lively presentation, given under a marquee, includes photos, utensils, antique vending machines, cacao bean sacks, and tropical plants. Not to be missed is a mouth-watering tour of the factory.

INDEX

P I C T U R E   C R E D I T S

Cover: Ryman and Cabannes/Top; p. 1 Scala; p. 2–3 J. P. Dieterlen; p. 4 Archiv für Kunst und Geschichte; p. 5 Sipa Icono; p. 6, 7 Kraft J. Suchard; p. 8 Lindt & Sprüngli (Schweiz) A.G.; p. 9 J. P. Dieterlen; p. 10 R.M.N./A.T.P.; p. 11, 12–13 J. Laiter; p. 14 C. Beaton/courtesy of Sotheby's; p. 15 Sipa Icono; p. 16 C. Pavard/Hoa-Qui; p. 17 G. De Laubier; p. 18 G. Planchenault; p. 19 R. Opie; p. 20 Bridgeman Art Library/O'Shea Gallery, London; p. 21 The Bettmann Archive; p. 22 N. and P. Mioulane/M.A.P.; p. 23 K. Mori/Image Bank; p. 24 Archiv für Kunst und Geschichte. 25 The Bettmann Archive; p. 26 O. Martel/Top; p. 27 J. L. Lénée/Hoa-Qui; p. 29 E. Valentin/Hoa-Qui; p. 30 G. Planchenault; p. 31, 32–33 G. De Laubier; p. 34 O. Martel/Top; p. 35 L. Jacquet; p. 36 Hulton Deutsch Collection; p. 37 Hawaiian Vintage; p. 38 S. Bimberg/National Geographic, Washington; p. 39 The Bettmann Archive; p. 40, 41 M. Riboud/Magnum Photos; p. 42, 43 J. Guillard/Scope; p. 44–45 G. Planchenault; p. 46 J. Guillard/Scope; p. 47 N. Cattlin/Holt Studios International; p. 48 G. De Laubier; p. 49 S. Salgado/Magnum Photos; p. 51 G. De Laubier; p. 52, 53, 54 N. Bruant/Allain François; p. 55 P. Schirnhofer/Stylograph; p. 56 Coll. Gismondi/photo; C. Germain; p. 57 Giraudon/Musée Condé, Chantilly; p. 58 G. Mobley/National Geographic, Washington; p. 59, 60 bottom Artephot/Oronoz; p. 60 bottom: Musée de l'Homme/photo: D. Destable; p. 61 Hulton Deutsch Collection; p. 62 top: Bibliothèque nationale; bottom: Musée de l'Homme/photo: D. Destable; p. 63 Luisa Ricciarini/Nimatallah; p. 64, 65 Artephot/Oronoz; p. 66 Luisa Ricciarini; p. 67 Hulton Deutsch Collection; p. 68 Giraudon/B.N.; p. 69 Cedus; bottom: Tropenmuseum/Amsterdam; p. 70 Musée de l'Homme/photo: D. Destable; p. 71 Hulton Deutsch Collection; p. 72 Giraudon/Musée des Beaux-Arts de Besançon; bottom: Hulton Deutsch Collection; p. 73 Droste Verlag/"Speise der Götter"; p. 74 Markus Senn Fotograf; p. 75 top: Roger-

Viollet/Boyer; bottom: Bibliothèque centrale du Museum d'histoire naturelle; p. 76 Hulton Deutsch Collection; p. 77 Giraudon/Ministère des DOM-TOM; p. 78 Museum of Ceramics, Barcelona/photo: R. Ricci; p. 79 Artephot/Oronoz; p. 80 The Hermitage/photo: Flammarion; p. 81 Cadbury Ltd/Bournville; bottom: Museum of Ceramics, Barcelona/photo: R. Ricci; p. 82 R.M.N./Château de Versailles; p. 83 Artephot/Oronoz; p. 84 Bibliothèque royale Albert 1er, Brussels; p. 85 top: Sterling and Francine Clark Art Institute; bottom: Caffè Florian, Venice; p. 86 Rapho; bottom: Museum of Ceramics, Barcelona/photo: R. Ricci; p. 87 Museum of London; p. 88 Giraudon/Musée du Louvre; p. 89 top: Artephot/photo: A.D.P.C.; bottom: Staatliche Museum zu Berlin/Preussischer Kulturbesitz Kunstgewerbemuseum; p. 90–91 Giraudon/Château de Versailles; p. 92 Archiv für Kunst und Geschichte; p. 93 Artothek/Artephot; p. 94 left: Photothèque des Musées de la Ville de Paris/Spadem; right and bottom: R.M.N./Musée du Louvre; p. 95 Coll. Callebaut; p. 96 Cedus; p. 97 top: J. L. Charmet; bottom: Staatliche Kunstsammlungen Dresden/photo: Richter; p. 98 J. L. Charmet/B.N.; bottom: Staatliche Kunstsammlungen Dresden/photo: Richter; p. 99 Bibliothèque des Arts décoratifs/Coll. Maciet; p. 100 G. Planchenault; p. 101 P. Moody Meyer/Stylograph; p. 102 J. Darblay; p. 103 top: Photothèque des Musées de la Ville de Paris/Spadem; bottom: Cedus; p. 104, 105 G. De Laubier; p. 106 Coll. Bonnat, Voiron; p. 107 J. P. Dieterlen; p. 108 J. P. Dieterlen; p. 109 H. Del Olmo/S.I.P.; p. 110 B. Touillon/S.I.P.; p. 111 Ryman and Cabannes/Top; p. 112 Cedus; p. 113 J. L. Charmet; p. 114 Archives Menier/photo: R. Jeetelle; p. 115 S. Couturier/Archipress; p. 116 top and 117 Ministère de la Culture et de la Francophonie/photo: P. Fortin/Inventaire Général/Spadem 1991/Nestlé France; bottom: Archives Menier, photo: R. Jeetelle; p. 118, 119 Cedus; p. 120, 121 bottom, Archives historiques Nestlé, Vevey; p. 121 top: Kraft J. Suchard;

p. 122 top: Cedus; bottom left and right: Kraft J. Suchard/photo: E. Gentil; p. 123 Kraft J. Suchard; p. 124, 125 and 126: Lindt & Sprüngli (Schweiz) A. G.; p. 126 Lindt & Sprüngli (Schweiz) A. G.; p. 127 top: Kraft J. Suchard/Eric Gentil; bottom: Lindt & Sprüngli (Schweiz) A. G.; p. 128 G. P. Cavallero/Horizons Editing; p. 129 J. P. Dieterlen; p. 130 Archives Caffarel; p. 131 top: C. Brusafferi/Cioccolata et Cie; bottom: Archives Majani; p. 132 Archives Majani; p. 133 Nestlé Archives, Vevey; p. 135 P. De Foy/Explorer; p. 136 top: J. L. Charmet; center: Archives Léonidas; bottom right: Coll. Callebaut; p. 137 Imhoff-Stollwerck Museum; p. 138 J. Stanfield/National Geographic, Washington; p. 139 C. Sarramon/Flammarion; p. 140–141 J. Stanfield/National Geographic, Washington; p. 142 Musée de la Publicité; p. 143 Edimedia; p. 144 top: P. Minamikawa/Sipa Press; bottom: Coll. Demel's, Vienna; p. 145 J. Laiter; p. 146 top: Giraudon; bottom: Imhoff-Stollwerck Museum; p. 147 Imhoff-Stollwerck Museum; p. 148 Hulton Deutsch Collection; p. 149 R. Opie; bottom: Cadbury Ltd, Bournville; p. 150 top: Hulton Deutsch Collection; bottom: R. Opie; p. 151 The Bettmann Archive; p. 152 top: Coll. Walter; bottom: Edimedia; p. 153 The Bettmann Archive; p. 154 P. Knaup./N. Le Fol; p. 155 J. P. Dieterlen; p. 156 Kraft J. Suchard; p. 157 Hulton Deutsch Collection; p. 158 Kobal Collection; p. 159 Hulton Deutsch Collection; p. 160 J. Laiter; p. 161 B. Touillon/S.I.P.; p. 162–163 J. Laiter; p. 164, 165 Kobal Collection; p. 167 J. Laiter; p. 168 P. Knaup; p. 169, 170–171, 172, 173; J. Laiter; p. 174 Hulton Deutsch Collection; p. 175 The Bettmann Archive; p. 176 J. Laiter; p. 177 P. Hussenot/Flammarion; p. 178 J. Laiter; p. 179 H. Del Olmo/S.I.P.; p. 181 J. P. Dieterlen; p. 183, 184 J. Laiter; p. 185 R. Beaufre/Top; p. 186 Ryman and Cabannes/Top; p. 187 P. Hussenot/Top; p. 188 Ryman and Cabannes Top; p. 192 J. P. Dieterlen; Back cover: P.Knaup.